FACILITATOR'S RESOURCE MANUAL FOR
Ethics in Action
INSTITUTIONAL VERSION

GERALD COREY
California State University, Fullerton
Diplomate in Counseling Psychology,
American Board of Professional Psychology

MARIANNE SCHNEIDER COREY
Private Practice and Consulting

ROBERT HAYNES
Borderline Productions

*Video directed by Thomas Walters
and produced by Robert Haynes*

BROOKS/COLE PUBLISHING COMPANY
I(T)P® An International Thomson Publishing Company

Pacific Grove • Albany • Belmont • Bonn • Boston • Cincinnati
Detroit • Johannesburg • London • Madrid • Melbourne • Mexico City
New York • Paris • Singapore • Tokyo • Toronto • Washington

Manual Credits
Sponsoring Editor: *Faith B. Stoddard*
Editorial Assistant: *Stephanie M. Andersen*
Production: *Dorothy Bell*
Cover Design: *Vernon T. Boes*
Cover Art: *Pat Scott*
Printing and Binding: *Patterson Printing*

COPYRIGHT © 1998 by Brooks/Cole Publishing Company
A division of International Thomson Publishing Inc.
I(T)P   The ITP logo is a registered trademark used herein under license.

For more information, contact:

BROOKS/COLE PUBLISHING COMPANY
511 Forest Lodge Road
Pacific Grove, CA 93950
USA

International Thomson Editores
Seneca 53
Col. Polanco
11560 México, D. F., México

International Thomson Publishing Europe
Berkshire House 168-173
High Holborn
London WC1V 7AA
England

International Thomson Publishing GmbH
Königswinterer Strasse 418
53227 Bonn
Germany

Thomas Nelson Australia
102 Dodds Street
South Melbourne, 3205
Victoria, Australia

International Thomson Publishing Asia
60 Albert Street
#15-01 Albert Complex
Singapore 189969

Nelson Canada
1120 Birchmount Road
Scarborough, Ontario
Canada M1K 5G4

International Thomson Publishing
Japan
Hirakawacho Kyowa Building, 3F
2-2-1 Hirakawacho
Chiyoda-ku, Tokyo 102
Japan

All rights reserved. Instructors of classes adopting *Ethics in Action*, by Corey, Corey, and Haynes, may reproduce material from this publication for classroom use. Otherwise, the text of this publication may not be reproduced, stored in a retrieval system, or transcribed, in any form or by any means—electronic, mechanical, photocopying, recording, or otherwise—without the prior written permission of the publisher, Brooks/Cole Publishing Company, Pacific Grove, California 93950.

Printed in the United States of America

10   9   8   7   6   5   4

ISBN 0-534-35620-6

CONTENTS

Program Overview	1
Synopsis of Videos	1
Learning Objectives	3
A Rationale for an Integrated Teaching/Learning Package	3
Ways of Teaching Ethical Decision Making	5
Sample Course Outline for an Ethics Course	11
Introducing the Video	17
Content Areas of the Institutional Version	
I. Ethical Decision Making	17
Multicultural Counseling Competencies: A Self Examination	30
II. Values and the Helping Relationship	35
III. Boundary Issues and Multiple Relationships	45
References	56
Other Books by the Coreys	60
Evaluation of *Ethics in Action*	62
How to Get More Information from Brooks/Cole	63

PROGRAM OVERVIEW

Students in counseling, social work, psychology, marriage and family therapy, nursing, and other helping professions encounter ethical dilemmas in clinical training and practice settings. Experienced clinicians as well struggle with ethical issues, often on a daily basis. Ethical issues are complex and multifaceted and defy simplistic cookbook solutions. Often there are no right or wrong answers in attempting to resolve ethical dilemmas. However, a strategy for problem-solving these dilemmas can help in the search for an answer. This unique video program addresses these ethical issues and provides problem-solving strategies for both new and experienced clinicians.

Ethics in Action is a new concept in ethics training programs. This video is designed to bring to life the ethical issues and dilemmas that counselors often encounter and provide ample opportunity for discussion, self-exploration and problem-solving of these issues and dilemmas. The Institutional Version of the video shows a weekend workshop co-led by Dr. Gerald Corey and Ms. Marianne Schneider Corey for a group of counseling students. The workshop included challenging questions and lively discussion, role-plays to bring the issues to life, and comments from the students and the Coreys. A Student Version accompanies the text and is designed to provide a self-study guide for the student in the ethics course.

This Facilitator's Resource Manual is designed to assist both the university instructor and the workshop leader as well. While this manual is written for the university instructor, the material contained herein may be adapted and modified to fit any clinical training situation, academic or applied.

SYNOPSIS OF VIDEOS

Ethics in Action: Institutional Version (60 minutes)
This video is divided into three segments: Ethical Decision Making, Values and the Helping Relationship, and Boundary Issues and Multiple Relationships. The first segment, Ethical Decision Making, examines the steps necessary in resolving ethical dilemmas and puts this model into practice through role-plays and discussion. The importance of self-awareness, as well as having a multicultural perspective, are also covered as these topics relate to becoming an ethical practitioner. The second segment, Values and the Helping Relationship, addresses the fact that every counselor has a value system which is likely to impact the counseling relationship. Common values influencing the counseling

process include those such as abortion, religion, sexual orientation, suicide, and the like. Again, role-plays and discussion bring the issues to life. The final segment, Boundary Issues and Multiple Relationships, addresses an ever-growing concern in practice regarding engaging in multiple roles and relationships with clients. Role-plays and discussion focus on topics such as managing boundaries, social relationships, sexual attraction, bartering, and gift-giving with clients.

Ethics in Action: Student Version (60 minutes)
This program covers many of the same topics found in the Institutional Version and more. The role-plays are all different from those in the Institutional Version and the student will find extensive opportunity to pause and work on their own response to each of the numerous situations presented. The Student Version is designed as homework for self-study or group-study while the Institutional Version is an ideal complement to the *Issues and Ethics in the Helping Professions* or to the *Becoming a Helper* texts, and the *Ethics in Action: Student Version*.

The Institutional Version is designed to be utilized over several class sessions. As the instructor, you may want to use this video in various ways. You may want to show the video all the way through and then go back and show one segment at a time and pause for discussion and group activities. Ideally, you would stop after each segment and have the class discuss the issues and the role-play and then embark on several role-plays enlisting class members to play the various roles. This can be followed by discussion which identifies the ethical issues, reviews the relevant codes and laws, and applies the eight-step decision-making model to a specific ethical dilemma. The class could then role-play various responses or approaches to the situation. The extensive discussion questions found later in this manual may be duplicated and used in part or in their entirety by the instructor. These questions may be given to students prior to viewing the video or utilized for group discussion when showing the videos in segments.

TARGET AUDIENCE

Ethics in Action is intended for students and practicing clinicians in any of the helping professions that encounter ethical issues and dilemmas. It is best utilized in conjunction with the following two books, both published by Brooks/Cole:
1. *Issues and Ethics in the Helping Professions* (5th edition, 1998) (Co-authored by Gerald Corey, Marianne Schneider Corey, and Patrick Callanan)
2. *Becoming a Helper* (3rd edition, 1998) (Co-authored by Marianne Schneider Corey and Gerald Corey)

LEARNING OBJECTIVES

After viewing the Institutional Video, viewers will be better able to:
1. Identify the more common ethical issues that counselors encounter.
2. Discuss the eight-step decision-making model designed to assist in resolving ethical dilemmas.
3. Discuss the importance of multicultural issues in ethics.
4. Discuss the value of self-awareness in knowing one's values and how they affect the counseling process.
5. Differentiate between exposing values and imposing values.
6. Recognize the importance of mananging boundaries and multiple roles in counseling practice.

A RATIONALE FOR AN INTEGRATED TEACHING/LEARNING PACKAGE

Why have an Institutional Version of the video *Ethics in Action*? It is clear that there are multiple intelligences and multiple learning styles. Some students learn best by listening to lectures and reading; others learn best by working on projects alone. Others prefer collaborative learning approaches, such as working in study groups while some learn more when they are participants in experiential learning (such as role-plays and group interaction), and some work best when they are presented with a problem situation and are challenged to figure out a solution. The following are examples of different styles of learning[1]:

- **Verbal-linguistic learners** have highly developed auditory skills, enjoy reading and writing, and are good at getting their point across.
- **Logical-mathematical learners** like to explore patterns and relationships, enjoy doing things in sequential order, and find it challenging to solve problems and use logical reasoning.
- **Visual-spatial learners** tend to be at home with the visual arts, maps, charts, and diagrams; often think in images and pictures; and can visualize clear images of things.

---

[1] For a more complete, yet basic discussion of the various learning styles, see Chapter 2 of *Living and Learning* (by G. Corey, C. Corey, and H. Corey, 1997, Wadsworth Publishing Company).

- **Musical-rhythmic learners** enjoy music and may prefer listening to music when they read or study.
- **Bodily-kinesthetic learners** need opportunities to move and act things out, and tend to respond best in classrooms that provide physical activities and hands-on learning.
- **Intrapersonal learners** tend to think creatively and independently, like to reflect on ideas, often prefer working independently rather than in groups, and may respond with strong opinions when controversial topics are discussed.
- **Interpersonal learners** learn best by relating, sharing, and participating in cooperative group environments; and enjoy interacting with others.

Recognizing the reality that there are multiple routes to learning, many instructors employ a diversity of teaching/learning strategies. There are certainly implications of the various styles of learning for the teaching of an ethics course. The integrated teaching/learning package that we are suggesting is based on the assumption that your students will best learn if a combination of approaches are built into your course. Ideally, this integrated package consists of the following:

- Students will have at least one main textbook for the course, plus some supplementary reading sources. Both the Institutional Video and the Student Video of *Ethics in Action* are geared to one of the following books as the basic textbook for your course: *Issues and Ethics in the Helping Professions* (5th edition, 1998), or *Becoming a Helper* (3rd edition, 1998).
- The Institutional Version of *Ethics in Action* can be shown in the various segments of your course as a way to promote other role-playing activities and to foster discussion and interaction. Of course, you have this Facilitator's Resource Manual to provide suggestions of how best to use each of the three parts of the Institutional Video.
- Students will have the Student Version of *Ethics in Action*, along with a Student Workbook designed to guide their learning and to assist them in a home study program. Both this video and the Student Workbook can be brought into the classroom as the basis for discussion.
- The videos provide a good model of how students can assume roles of both client and counselor, as they creatively act out problem situations. The videos will bring to life a range of problematic situations that challenge students to think about ethical alternatives.
- In addition to traditional teaching approaches—reading, lectures, discussion, small groups, guest speakers, field trips, writing papers, taking tests—your

class can include an experiential component where students enact situations depicting ethical concerns.

WAYS OF TEACHING ETHICAL DECISION MAKING

What follows are some ideas for the teaching of ethics and suggestions for incorporating experiential approaches into ethics courses, especially the use of role-play and involvement in case vignettes.

Kitchener (1986) has suggested that ethics training should create sensitivity to the ethical issues in the profession and to the implications of professional actions; should improve the ability to reason about ethical issues; should instill the determination to act in ethical ways; and should teach tolerance of ambiguity in ethical decision making as opposed to rigid indoctrination of "right" and "wrong."

We endorse the practice of teaching students the process of making ethical decisions from the very beginning of their training program. The teaching of ethics can be conceptualized as progressing from a focus on theoretical issues to a stress on practical issues. When students are introduced to ethics education, it is likely that the emphasis will be on teaching general principles of ethical reasoning. Specific application can involve creating situations in the classroom in which students are challenged to apply ethical principles to specific cases.

TRENDS IN TEACHING OF PROFESSIONAL ETHICS

The process of learning to become an ethical practitioner begins with counselor-education programs, which normally include seminars in ethical principles and practices. Students should, as a beginning, thoroughly familiarize themselves with established ethical standards. They need to be sensitive to any ethical problems that arise in their practicum experiences and then discuss the problems in a seminar session or consult their supervisor. Part of a counselor's training is developing a sense of sound judgment, and dealing with basic ethical issues can assist in that development.

Fortunately, there is a clear trend toward introducing counselors-in-training to the kinds of ethical and legal issues that they are likely to encounter. In reviewing the state of ethical training for counseling psychology doctoral students, Wilson and Ranft (1993) concluded that ethics training in graduate psychology programs has blossomed in the last decade. The results of their survey indicated that 94% of counseling psychology programs require training in ethics. Students in these programs feel prepared for both ethical and legal issues that are likely to arise in their professional roles. They claim that they feel more prepared in the decision-making process than in factual information of ethics.

The increased interest given to ethics education is (in part) related to an increase in malpractice litigation. The greater consciousness in the human services professions about ethical and legal responsibilities parallels a concurrent rise in public consciousness about legal rights. There is a great deal of professional concern over identifying appropriate actions in the face of conflicting ethical, legal, and professional demands (Haas, Malouf, & Mayerson, 1986).

Most of the attention has been given to violations of confidentiality and to sexual intimacies with clients. Other types of unethical behaviors have been documented, however, such as misrepresentation of skills, problems in the methods of collecting fees, improper use of assessment techniques, faulty diagnosis, treatment error, failure to respect client integrity, inappropriate public statements, violation of civil rights, assault and battery, and unethical research practices (Lipsitz, 1985; Pope, 1986).

A trend that we would like to see in the teaching of ethics is for educators to demonstrate a willingness to engage in open discussion with their students about their own ethical beliefs. We would also hope that educators would realize the value of teaching ethical behavior through the process of modeling ethical practices by the way they relate to students in their classes.

It is our view that formal course work in ethics, both in separate courses and through an integrated approach with the rest of the curriculum, will significantly help students benefit from supervised fieldwork. The course work can alert students to ethical, legal, and professional issues that they might not have looked for, and they will be able to bring to their fieldwork questions about the ethical dimensions of their practice.

THE FORMATION OF AN ETHICAL SENSE

For students, developing an ethical sense includes committing themselves to their education, being an active learner, learning from role models such as their professors, and getting involved in related course work. From our perspective the cultivation of an ethical sense begins with students' commitment to their education in the helping professions. The way they approach their education has a bearing on the way they will approach their professional career. If they are committed to their studies on both an intellectual and emotional level, they will probably bring this enthusiasm and dedication to their professional practice. Of course, there are those students who are committed to manipulating the system so that they can merely get by with minimal effort. Some take the shortest route to earning a degree and getting a license, and once they attain these goals, they stop learning. We are convinced that these people are limited in their capacity to help others.

In addition to being an active learner, we think it is essential that students be aware of their motivations for choosing the helping professions as a career. The motivations for being a helper are related to the development of an ethical sense. Although many personal needs can be met through helping others, it is crucial that these needs not be met at the expense of the client. Those who make a lifetime commitment to helping others have a responsibility to be clear about what they are getting from their work and how their personal characteristics play a vital role in their ability to make appropriate ethical decisions.

We contend that the faculty of any program in the helping professions plays a major role in modeling an ethical sense. The ways in which the faculty members teach their courses and relate to and supervise students have a significant impact. For example, supervisors may model confidentiality or the lack of it by how they talk about their own clients. As Kitchener (1984) has pointed out, one way of teaching students what it means to be an ethical professional is by being truthful, honest, and direct with them. The faculty members must be open to honest self-exploration of the ethical issues they face if they hope to have an impact on their students' ability to think from an ethical perspective.

A PERSONAL PERSPECTIVE ON THE TEACHING OF ETHICS FROM JERRY COREY

At California State University, Fullerton, I typically teach both an undergraduate course in ethical and professional issues for the Human Services Department and a graduate course in ethics in counseling for the Counseling Department. [See my sample course outline that follows this section.]

Rather than rely on lecture methods, I do my best to involve both undergraduate and graduate students in identifying and examining the basic ethical principles involved in a variety of ethical dilemmas. Toward the goal of increasing student involvement, I encourage role-playing as a way to bring ethical dilemmas to life. Frequently, I assume the role of devil's advocate and challenge students to come up with reasons for whatever position they might assume. The students are encouraged to bring their concerns about the issues in the assigned readings and the videos. As much as possible, I attempt to facilitate interaction and discussion within the classroom. I hope that students will develop an appreciation for the value of thinking through ethical dilemmas by examining their own motivations and values. I ask students to be alert to the subtle ways that they might be ethically insensitive at times. I consistently encourage them to focus on their own motivations and behavior, rather than developing a judgmental stance by critiquing the ethics of others. Although many of my students do not have much practical experience in the field, the use of practical examples, cases involving ethical dilemmas, and role-playing of scenarios do help students to gain a sense of the challenges that they will eventually encounter. Through feedback from my students, I continue to find involvement in a variety of role-play situations and discussing case vignettes to be an effective way of developing decision-making attitudes and skills.

As the instructor, we encourage you to take the initiative by playing the role of client in various situations depicting ethical dilemmas. By role-playing the client, you can present students with all sorts of subtle twists to a situation involving an ethical issue. You'll also be modeling for your students and showing them how they can get involved in similar enactments. Not only can your students create variations of the role-plays that they view in the videos, but they can enact some of the open-ended cases that are presented in the textbook.

As an alternative, you can give your students a handout with several role-plays for a particular topic that will require them to learn through role-playing. Or, your students can form small groups and bring in some of their own ethical situations that they would like to enact and then discuss. The possibilities for role-play are almost endless, and this method can be used as a way to introduce a topic or to facilitate an exciting discussion among the students.

In the ethics classes I teach, I play the roles of both client and therapist. However, I do my best to get students to try on the role of therapist first, and usually ask for several students to portray different ways of dealing with a case. This is done to promote the idea that, because ethical dilemmas are complex, there are usually a number of approaches that can be used in working toward a resolution. Acting in the role of therapist, even if students demonstrate a "wrong way" or a questionable way of dealing with the situation, much learning can occur when we get into the discussion after the role-play. When I do enter into a role-play as a therapist, I generally do so after students have tried their hand in dealing with the problem. Even then, I present this as my perspective on the topic, rather than the "right approach."

My colleagues and I consistently find that when we do workshops with professionals, or when we teach courses for undergraduate or graduate students in the helping professions, that they eventually become less self-conscious the more we work with ethical issues through role-play. It does help to assure students that it is acceptable to make mistakes, and that they will learn a great deal more if they are willing to put themselves into situations through experiential activities. On the next page are some examples of student perceptions about ethics courses that attempt to bring ethical dilemmas alive through the process of role-play.

STUDENT PERCEPTIONS OF AN ETHICS COURSE

Students enrolled in ethics courses that I have taught have made comments such as the following about how their course has been instrumental in acquiring ethical decision-making attitudes and skills:

- I was frustrated because I wasn't given answers in the course. All my answers came within myself.
- I have learned that the line between right and wrong is not always clear or straight, but is often fuzzy and blurred. I have learned to not be so quick to judge another person's ethics, but to concentrate on discovering what is right for myself.
- As a result of taking this course, it was interesting seeing how my views changed from the beginning to the end of the course.
- This ethics class actually challenged me to re-evaluate what I thought I believed and introduced me to some possibilities that I never would have considered before.
- The course was extremely useful in helping me better understand a particular issue presented and in preparing me to deal with real issues.
- I learned to appreciate the reality that there are few clear-cut answers in ethics, and the course raises more questions than gives answers.
- I am beginning to realize that the field of counseling is much more complicated than most people think. It seems there are very few easy answers. Most decisions and choices are some shade of gray instead of black and white.
- I realized that there is a lot more to being an ethical counselor than memorizing the codes.
- The class discussions promoted a lot of growth and thought-provoking disagreements.
- I learned the importance of looking at my own behavior for the potential of unethical behavior, rather than focusing on the ethical practices of others.
- Rather than just memorizing facts, the course stirred me emotionally and made me think. The course helped me clarify my personal values and at the same time made me more comfortable with dealing with ambivalence and issues that have no easy answers.
- In this course I learned to pinpoint issues of concern to me and became more aware of my positions on an ethical problem.
- I was challenged to personalize the material and to develop my own ideas instead of embracing the position of others.

- I was stimulated to think about options that I hadn't considered or hadn't been aware of. Working with the cases allowed me the opportunity to try on attitudes and positions to see what I thought about them.
- The most significant learnings for me that grew out of this course are: (1) the solidification of my own values, (2) an appreciation for the necessity of my own personal counseling experience, (3) a deep respect for the ethical responsibility I will have as a counselor, and (4) coming to the realization that the education I receive at this university only meets the minimum standard.

SAMPLE COURSE OUTLINE FOR AN ETHICS COURSE

I'm providing an abbreviated version of the course outline that I use for a graduate ethics course in the Counseling Department. I also teach this course in a similar way with similar content for an undergraduate course in the Human Services Department—both at California State University at Fullerton. This course outline shows how I integrate both the Institutional and Student videos, *Ethics in Action*, into the basic framework of the class.

COUNSELING 526 [3 Units]
PROFESSIONAL, ETHICAL, AND LEGAL ISSUES IN COUNSELING

Dr. Jerry Corey, *Professor of Counseling and Human Services*

COURSE DESCRIPTION
Prerequisites: Counseling 520, 521, and 522. Ethical and legal standards as related to critical professional issues. The relationship and integration of values for the counselor's role in practice, training, supervision, and consultation.

REQUIRED READINGS FOR COUNSELING 526
1. Corey, G., Corey, M., & Callanan, P. (1998). *Issues and Ethics in the Helping Professions* (5th ed.). Pacific Grove, CA: Brooks/Cole.
2. *Herlihy, B., & Corey, G. (1996). *ACA Ethical Standards Casebook.* ACA Publication.
3. *Herlihy, B., & Corey, G. (1997). *Boundary Issues in Counseling: Multiple Roles and Responsibilities.* ACA Publication.
4. Student video on *Ethics in Action* (Brooks/Cole) along with a Student Workbook. There is also an Institutional Version of the *Ethics in Action* video, which will be shown in class. The Student video and the Institutional video are different videos, although they deal with the same content, and both videos supplement the readings for this course.

*Both of these books are available in the Limited Loan Library (for one-day checkout), so it is not necessary to purchase them.

COUNSELING 526 SCHEDULE

WEEKS	TOPICS FOR DISCUSSION AND ASSIGNED READINGS
Week 1	**Introduction to Professional Ethics** Chapter 1—Self-Inventory (Discuss in class) Videos: *ACA Tele-Conference on Ethics in Counseling* and *Ethics in Action* video (Part One: Ethical Decisions)
Week 2	**Counselor and Person as Professional** Complete reading of both Chapters 1 and 2 Video: *Ethics in Action* (Part One: Ethical Decisions)
Week 3	**Chapter 3: Values and the Helping Relationship** Review the Codes of Ethics in Appendix **Take-Home Quiz** on Chapters 1, 2, 3 due today Video: *Ethics in Action* (Part Two: Values)
Week 4	**Chapter 4: Client Rights and Counselor Responsibilities** Legal Issues and Malpractice Concerns *ACA Casebook* (Read selected essays on above topics) Video: *ACA Ethics Video* (Part on Informed Consent and Confidentiality) **Take-Home Quiz** on Chapter 4 due
Week 5	**Chapter 5: Confidentiality: Ethical and Legal Issues** *ACA Casebook* (Read selected essays on above topics) **Take-Home Quiz** on Chapter 5 due • Paper #1 due
Week 6	**Chapter 6: Theory, Practice, and Research** *ACA Casebook* (Read selected essays on above topics) • Mid-Term Test on Chapters 1 to 6
Week 7	**Chapter 7: Managing Boundaries and Multiple Roles and Relationships** Videos: *ACA Ethics Video* (Part on Dual Relationships) and *Ethics in Action* (Part Three: Boundary Issues) **Take-Home Quiz** on Chapters 6 and 7 due
Week 8	**Boundary Issues in Counseling: Multiple Roles** Reading due: Herlihy & Corey: *Boundary Issues in Counseling* Video: *Ethics in Action* (Part Three: Boundary Issues)
Week 9	**Chapter 8: Professional Competence and Training** *Boundary Issues* book Chapter 4 (Counselor Ed) **Take-Home Quiz** on Chapter 8 due
Week 10	**Chapter 9: Issues in Supervision and Consultation** *ACA Casebook* (Read selected essays on above topics)

	Boundary Issues book Chapter 5 (Supervision) **Take-Home Quiz** on Chapter 9 due
Week 11	**Chapter 10: Multicultural Perspectives and Diversity** *ACA Casebook* Video: *ACA Ethics Video* (Part Three: Ethics in Multicultural Counseling) **Take-Home Quiz** on Chapter 10 due
Week 12	**Chapter 11: The Counselor in the Community** *Boundary Issues* book Chapter 7 (Community) **Take-Home Quiz** on Chapter 11 due • Paper #2 due
Week 13	**Chapter 12: Ethics in Marriage and Family Therapy** *Boundary Issues* book Chapter 8 (Family Counseling) **Take-Home Quiz** on Chapter 12 due
Week 14	**Chapter 13: Ethics in Group Counseling** *Boundary Issues* book Chapter 6 (Preparation of Group Counselors) **Take-Home Quiz** on Chapter 13 due
Week 15	**Student Presentations** and **Review of Issues and Evaluation**
Week 16	**Final Examination** Final Exam covers Chapters 7 to 13 of *Issues and Ethics* (100 questions); *ACA Casebook* (100 questions). Final exam consists of a total of 200 objective-type questions.

COURSE RATIONALE

Although professional counselors need to operate under personal and professional codes of ethics, often these guidelines leave many questions unanswered. No single universally "right" answer exists for most ethical dilemmas. As graduate students in counseling, it is critical to be familiarized with the current professional, ethical, and legal issues that confront the counselor's role in a variety of settings. It is especially important to become sensitive to thinking about different ethical dilemmas and to learn decision-making strategies. Rather than arriving at clear answers, what is important is to learn how to think through ethical issues in a systematic manner.

COURSE OBJECTIVES

1. To familiarize the student with the profession's ethical standards and practice.
2. To familiarize the student with California laws for counselors and psychotherapists.
3. To examine the role of ethics and values in the counseling process.

4. To acquaint the student with various counselor roles and the potential for the development of ethical dilemmas.
5. To facilitate awareness of current professional issues facing the field.
6. To enhance the student's development of professional identity and its associated responsibilities.
7. To examine the counselor functions of supervision, appraisal, consultation, and research in relation to values and ethical standards.
8. To examine the ethical decision-making process and its role in the counseling process.
9. To assist the student in examining, critiquing, and articulating her or his own ethical posture.

COURSE COMPETENCIES

1. The student will be able to respond to ethical dilemmas by a decision-making process.
2. The student will be able to communicate an understanding of the laws for counselors and psychotherapists in California.
3. The student will be able to identify the different major components of ethical codes for professional counselors.
4. The student will be able to communicate how her/his personal values influence her/his ethical posture.
5. The student will be able to identify the professional organizations for counselors.

FOCUS OF THE ETHICS COURSE

The class will *not* be a lecture class, rather it will be conducted more along the lines of a *seminar*. While some brief lectures will be given, the focus is upon discussion, interaction, role-playing, exploration of issues, and carrying out in class (and small groups) the *activities and exercises* at the end of each chapter. Come to class prepared! Read, think, be willing to state your views, exchange ideas!

GRADING PRACTICES AND POLICY

Your grade for this course will be determined by evidence of the quality of your learning as demonstrated by your performance below:

(1) **Paper #1** will count as 25% of your course grade.
(2) **Paper #2** will count as 25% of your course grade.
(3) **Take-home QUIZZES** (100 points) and **MID-TERM EXAM** (100 points), for a total of 200 points counts as 25% of your course grade.

(4) **FINAL EXAMINATION** consists of 200 objective-type questions from two texts—*Issues and Ethics in the Helping Professions* (Chapters 7-13) [100 questions] and *ACA Ethics Casebook*, [100 questions] for a total of 200 points and counts as 25% of your course grade.

NOTE: Be sure to bring TEXTBOOKS, Readings, and this COURSE OUTLINE and SYLLABUS to each of the classes. Do all of the required reading prior to the day that we'll be discussing a specific topic. Also, view the STUDENT VIDEO of ETHICS IN ACTION and complete the exercises in the STUDENT WORKBOOK prior to the class sessions that deal with these topics: Ethical decision making; values and the helping relationship; and boundary issues and multiple relationships.

Class Participation: This course is organized in a seminar format and you are expected to participate in the class activities and discussions. Your final course grade may be affected by both the quality and quantity of your in-class participation and attendance. If you are not willing to become an active participant, do not enroll in the course.

ATTENDANCE is expected at each class meeting, unless you have an emergency situation or are really ill. For me to credit you with an EXCUSED ABSENCE, you need to know that it is YOUR RESPONSIBILITY to inform me of such cases immediately upon returning to class. Absences will be a factor in determining your participation/attendance grade; excessive absences might result in getting a full grade deducted (or in some cases even failing the course). While I do not mean to be petty about this issue, I do expect you to function as a professional in any agency, which means showing up and participating!

Grading Scale (percentage) is as follows:
100-98 = A+
97-94 = A
93-91 = A-
90-88 = B+
87-84 = B
83-81 = B-
80-78 = C+
77-74 = C
73-71 = C-
70-68 = D+
67-64 = D
63-61 = D-
Below 60 = F

A curve is not used for grading in this course. Students who choose to remain in this course until the end tend to do well. The grade of "A" is reserved for exception performance in all of the areas of the course.

GUIDELINES FOR PAPER #1 AND PAPER #2 FOR COUNSELING 526

PAPERS #1 AND #2 make up 50% of your course grade. *LATE PAPERS* generally have a **penalty of at least** -15% deduction (if only a few days late) from the total. They should be TYPED and double-spaced, CAREFULLY PROOFREAD, and should give evidence of considerable thought/outside reading, and must show a development of your positions in a coherent, logical, and organized way. Approximate length: **Each of your papers is to be between 10 to 12 pages.**

For **PAPER #1**, the central theme is a **VALUE ISSUES PAPER**. This paper is to be approximately **10 to 12 pages** in length. In this paper your task is to examine ways your values might affect your counseling practice. Use Chapter 3 (Values) as the core chapter, but do relate the discussion of your values to some of the other topics covered in the readings in Chapters 1 through 5. Focus on ways that your values would influence the manner in which you think about ethical issues and how you would resolve an ethical dilemma. Identify some of your core values and show how these values could either enhance or inhibit the effectiveness of counseling. You might also address implications of your values for the informed consent process. How might your values influence your perspective on client rights and your responsibilities as a counselor (subject of Chapter 4)? How might your values influence your decisions with respect to confidentiality concerns (subject of Chapter 5)? How does the person you are have implications for you as a professional (Chapter 2)? This is to be a personal reflection and position paper, so explore your values in light of the practical implications for your future counseling practice.

For **PAPER #2** the central theme is **BOUNDARY ISSUES IN COUNSELING**. Draw heavily from the *Boundary Issues* text and Chapter 7 of *Issues and Ethics*. As with the first paper, this paper should be approximately **10 to 12 pages** in length. Address your thoughts on the topics of multiple relationships and multiple responsibilities, with an emphasis on a discussion of boundary concerns you might wrestle with—and how you can take steps toward managing boundaries. Show how boundary concerns apply in the following areas: counseling practice; education and training; supervision; consultation; multicultural perspectives; community work; marital and family therapy; and group counseling.

INTRODUCING THE VIDEO

For the most part, the cast in the video consists of graduate students in counseling or social work at various universities who are bringing ethical dilemmas to life through role-plays and then discussing their views on ethical issues. This was a part of a three-day workshop on "Ethics in the Helping Professions." The role-plays that are depicted represent many of the typical ethical situations that beginning counselors encounter.

We want to stress that the students are role-playing in all situations, not depicting their own real-life issues. Also, in the therapist's role, the students are not necessarily demonstrating appropriate, ethical, and effective interventions. In the commentary, the Coreys and the students discuss each role-play. Our attempt is to present various approaches to dealing with ethical situations, rather than to demonstrate the best way of dealing with the situations. Some of the role-plays illustrate sound ethical practices, while others are questionable at best. In a number of cases, the students role-playing the therapist are imposing their values or revealing their own countertransference. This video is designed to provoke thought and stimulate discussion of the issues. Both the Facilitator's Resource Manual and the Student Workbook provide discussion, analysis, and commentary on each of the role-plays.

CONTENT AREAS FOR THE INSTITUTIONAL VERSION

SEGMENT ONE: ETHICAL DECISION MAKING
Ethical decision making is best thought of as a process. A good follow up to this segment of the video is to ask students to discuss what process they would go through in their attempt to resolve any ethical dilemmas they might face.

REFERENCES
This Facilitator's Resource Manual is geared primarily to the Institutional Version of the video, *Ethics in Action*. Throughout this manual, we will be making references to the following two textbooks as they apply to the topics addressed in the video program:
1. *Issues and Ethics in the Helping Professions* (5th Edition, 1998). (Co-authored by Gerald Corey, Marianne Schneider Corey, and Patrick Callanan and published by Brooks/Cole Publishing Company).

2. *Becoming a Helper* (3rd Edition, 1998). (Co-authored by Marianne Schneider Corey and Gerald Corey and published by Brooks/Cole Publishing Company).

KEY POINTS IN SEGMENT ONE

We make points in the video about the complexity of ethical decision making, and how there are no easy answers. As instructors, you may want to emphasize points such as those listed below on the topic of making ethical decisions.

- There are few simple answers to complex ethical problems.
- Rather than thinking in terms of "the one right answer," think more about the best answer you can come up with, along with the reasons for your decision.
- Know the codes of ethics and follow them, but don't expect codes to provide you with the specific answer to a dilemma you are facing.
- Realize that there may be several appropriate courses of action for the same ethical dilemma. Various professionals will have different perspectives and may resolve an issue differently.
- It is good to remember that each of us is responsible and accountable for the consequences of our decisions.
- In making ethical decisions it is essential to consider what is best for the client—but also to consider the impact of the decision on the practitioner, on others in the client's life, on society, and on the profession.
- Becoming an ethical practitioner is not something that is accomplished once and for all.
- Be prepared to reexamine ethical issues throughout the course of your professional career. Refinement of these issues is an ongoing process.

REFERENCES

1. Refer to *Becoming a Helper* (pp. 116–120) on ethical decision making, professional codes and making ethical decisions, and an ethical decision-making model.
2. Refer to *Issues and Ethics*, (Chapter 1, pp. 2–3) for additional points to address for this segment of the program.

You might want to give students some kind of self-inventory to assess (1) their beliefs and attitudes pertaining to the process of ethical decision making, and (2) their thoughts about some of the topics that are covered in this video program. You could use parts of the self-inventories in the textbooks below:
1. *Becoming a Helper* (pp. 115–116)
2. *Issues and Ethics* (pp. 19–29)

STEPS IN THE ETHICAL DECISION-MAKING PROCESS: The Role of Codes of Ethics in Making Decisions

Raise the question: Do the codes provide answers to dilemmas?
1. Refer to *Issues and Ethics* (Chapter 1, pp. 6–8) on the discussion of the role of professional codes. See *Becoming a Helper* (pp. 118–119) on role of codes in ethical decision making.

Some points to bring out in addressing the question of the role professional codes play in resolving ethical dilemmas are:
- Most codes of the various professions are broad and general, rather than precise and specific.
- Some issues cannot be handled as simply as consulting the codes.
- At times codes may conflict with the law or with institutional policies and practices.
- Ethical codes need to be interpreted in light of cultural perspectives.
- Codes provide guidance, but they are not a blueprint that removes all need for using judgment and ethical reasoning.
- The majority of unethical behavior is difficult to detect. Ethics codes are, therefore, difficult to enforce. This places primary responsibility on the self-monitoring process of the counselor.

Suggestion: You might want to reproduce at least one of the professional organization's code of ethics (or a portion of the codes), so that your students will become familiar with the general areas addressed in a typical ethics code. In the Appendix of *Issues and Ethics* (pp. 443–507) the following ethics codes are given:
A. *Codes of Ethics and Standards of Practice*, American Counseling Association (ACA, 1995)
B. *Ethical Principles of Psychologists and Code of Conduct*, American Psychological Association (APA, 1995)
C. *Code of Ethics*, National Association of Social Workers (NASW, 1996)
D. *AAMFT Code of Ethics*, American Association of Marriage and Family Therapy (AAMFT, 1991)
E. *Ethical Standards of Human Service Professionals*, National Organization for Human Service Education (NOHSE, 1995)

OTHER REFERENCES

At the end of this Facilitator's Resource Manual are a list of references that you'll probably find useful to provide additional lecture and discussion material.

We will indicate a number of these references throughout this Facilitator's Resource Guide at each of the various segments.

In preparing for your class on the topic of the ethical decision-making process, you may want to consult other sources besides *Issues and Ethics* and *Becoming a Helper*. See the sources below.

Herlihy, B., & Corey, G. (1996a). *ACA ethical standards casebook* (5th ed.). Alexandria, VA: American Counseling Association.

> Refer to Introduction (pp. 3–15) for relevant points to this part of the video program. Presented here is a discussion of foundational principles of codes of ethics, developing a personal ethical stance, and an ethical decision-making model.

Herlihy, B., & Corey, G. (1997a). *Boundary issues in counseling: Multiple roles and responsibilities*. Alexandria, VA: American Counseling Association.

> In this book, Chapter 3 (The Client's Perspective) is especially relevant. See Susan Walden's (1997) article in this chapter on pages 40–47.

Herlihy, B., & Corey, G. (1997b). Codes of ethics as catalysts for improving practice. In *The Hatherleigh guide to ethics in therapy* (pp. 39–59). New York: Hatherleigh Press.

> In this last source, Herlihy and Corey identify three basic purposes of ethics codes: education, accountability, and improving practice.
> - Codes educate counseling professionals and the general public about our responsibilities.
> - Codes provide a mechanism for professional accountability, and, through their enforcement, protect clients from unethical practices.
> - Codes can serve as a basis for self-monitoring and improving practice.

HOW TO THINK ABOUT ETHICS

Raise the question: What steps would you take in making a decision involving an ethical dilemma?

In this video we talk about steps in ethical decision making. We ask, "If you were confronted with an ethical dilemma, what would you do?" In our classes, we open a discussion involving students on the topic of how they think about ethics and how they expect they would proceed in working through an ethical problem. It is sometimes helpful to give them a brief situation and ask them what steps they would take in dealing with it.

See *Issues and Ethics* (Chapter 1, pp. 15–17); also refer to *Becoming a Helper* (Chapter 5, pp. 118–120).

KEY POINTS

A few key points that we make in this segment of the program include:

- The top consideration is to think about what will be in the best interests of your client.
- In making ethical decisions, when appropriate, include your client in this ethical decision-making process.
- The key is to make ethical decisions *with* clients, not simply *for* them. Actively involve clients in the process to the extent that is possible and appropriate.
- Realize that there may be many appropriate options when you are faced with deciding on an ethical course of action.
- Ask for feedback before you decide to carry out a particular plan. You don't need to struggle with how best to deal with an ethical dilemma alone. Seek out fellow students, supervisors, and colleagues, and be willing to share ideas.
- The steps in making an ethical decision are not linear. In essence, the eight-step model below is a circular one. It may be necessary to go back to earlier steps for further information or more exploration.

EIGHT STEPS IN MAKING ETHICAL DECISIONS

Refer to *Becoming a Helper* (pp. 119–120) and *Issues and Ethics* (pp. 15–17) for the specific details on these steps.

Below are eight steps with suggested questions to raise for class discussion on how students would accomplish the tasks for each of these steps.

1. Identify the problem or dilemma.
   - Is this an ethical, legal, moral, professional, or clinical problem?
   - Is it a combination of more than one of these?
   - How can you know the nature of the problem?
   - Would you consult at this early stage as you are identifying the problem?
   - How might you begin the process of consultation with your client about the nature of the problem?
2. Identify the potential issues involved.
   - How might you best evaluate the rights, responsibilities, and welfare of all those involved and those who are affected by the decision, including your own welfare as a practitioner?
   - How can you best promote your client's independence and self-determination?
   - What actions have the least chance of bringing harm to your client?
   - What decision will best safeguard the client's welfare?

- How can you create a trusting and collaborative climate where your clients can find their own answers?
- What principles can you use in prioritizing the potential issues involved in this situation?

3. Review the relevant ethical codes.
   - What guidance can you find on the specific problem under review by consulting with the professional codes?
   - Are your values in agreement with the specific ethical code in question?
   - How clear and specific are the codes on the specific area under consideration?

4. Know the applicable laws and regulations.
   - Are there any laws or regulations that have a bearing on the situation under consideration?
   - What are the specific and relevant state and federal laws that apply to the ethical dilemma?

5. Obtain consultation.
   - Assuming that you will consult with a colleague or a supervisor, what would you expect from this consultation?
   - What kinds of questions do you want to ask of those with whom you consult?
   - With whom do you seek consultation? Do you consult only with those who share your orientation, or do you look for consultants with different perspectives?
   - How can you use the consultation process as an opportunity to test the justification of a course of action you are inclined to take?
   - What kinds of information do you document when you consult?

6. Consider possible and probable courses of action.
   - What are some ways that you can brainstorm many possible courses of action?
   - Are you willing to involve your client in the discussion of the various courses of action?
   - What might you document pertaining to discussions with your client about probable courses of action?

7. Enumerate the consequences of various decisions.
   - How can you best evaluate the potential consequences of each course of action, before implementing a particular action plan?
   - Are you willing to involve your client in the discussion of the implications of each course of action for the client?

- What ethical principles can you use as a framework for evaluating the consequences of a given course of action?
8. Decide on what appears to be the best course of action.
    - After carefully considering all the information you have gathered, how do you know what seems to be the best action to take?
    - Do you solicit the input of your client in making this decision at this phase?
    - Once you have formulated a plan of action, do you ask for feedback from a colleague or supervisor?
    - Once the course of action has been implemented, what are some ways that you might evaluate the course of action?
    - Are you willing to follow up to determine the outcomes and see if further action is necessary?

BASIC MORAL PRINCIPLES IN MAKING ETHICAL DECISIONS

In addition to discussing the specific steps in the ethical decision-making process, we suggest introducing students to the difference between mandatory ethics and aspirational ethics. Refer to *Issues and Ethics* (p. 5).

Also, this would be a good time to present the six basic moral principles that form the foundation of functioning at the highest level of ethical functioning (aspirational ethical practice). Refer to *Issues and Ethics* (pp. 12–14) for a discussion of the following six moral principles underlying the process of making ethical decisions:

1. **Autonomy:** the promotion of self-determination, or the freedom of clients to choose their own direction.
2. **Nonmaleficence:** avoiding doing harm, which includes refraining from actions that risk hurting clients, either intentionally or unintentionally.
3. **Beneficence:** doing good for others.
4. **Justice:** fairness, or providing equal treatment to all people.
5. **Fidelity:** making honest promises and honoring these commitments to clients.
6. **Veracity:** truthfulness.

In addition to assisting your students in applying the steps in the ethical decision-making model, ask them to discuss the implications of the role-play situations in this video from the perspective of the basic moral principles.

IMPORTANCE OF THE DOCUMENTATION PROCESS

In the video we underscore the importance of documenting the steps taken in thinking through and resolving an ethical dilemma. Although documentation is not strictly an ethical concern, there are significant legal ramifications of the documentation process. Indeed, from a legal perspective, if an action has not been documented, then it has not been taken!

This might be a good time to open the discussion of documentation with your students. Refer to the *Issues and Ethics* book on Record Keeping, in Chapter 4 on pages 125–127. See also pages 145–149 on documentation as a strategy for protection against a malpractice suit.

From *Becoming a Helper*, you may want to introduce ideas for ways to prevent malpractice suits. This discussion is given in Chapter 5 on pages 148–150.

ANALYSIS AND FOLLOW-UP DISCUSSION OF THE ROLE-PLAYS

(Note: The times given for each role-play are approximate running times from the beginning of the Brooks/Cole logo at the start of the tape to the start of the role-play.)

The first role-play, "Following Me," (6:50) pertains to a counselor who recognizes that she is beyond her level of competence and considers referral of a client who appears to be delusional. When the client reports that others are following her, the counselor expresses her concern to the client and attempts to get her to see a more qualified professional.

QUESTIONS FOR CLASS DISCUSSION

- What did you think of the therapist's way of working with her client?
- What might you have said or done differently?
- If you were the client in this situation, how do you imagine you would have felt?

In *Becoming a Helper* refer to the section on Recognizing Competence and Learning to Refer (pp. 121–122).

See also *Issues and Ethics*, (Chapter 8, pp. 266–270) on Therapist Competence, and also on the topic of making referrals. In this book (on page 267) we reprint the professional codes of ethics on competence. Clearly, all of these codes specify how essential it is to practice only within the boundaries of one's competence.

Within the context of the codes dealing with competence, open a discussion around these questions:

- What would you do if you were the therapist in this case? If your client indicated that she was convinced that people were following her, would you feel competent to deal with her?
- If you determined that you did not have the education and training necessary to competently deal with your client, what might you do?
- Would you suggest a referral? If you did attempt to refer this client, and she refused, indicating that she liked and trusted you, what might you do then?
- How might your need to have your client like you influence your decision to refer her, if you believed that you did not have the competence to deal with her?
- At least two basic moral principles apply to this case: (1) What actions would most promote the client's welfare (beneficence)? and (2) If the counselor realizes she has reached the limits of her competence, yet continues seeing the client, are her actions ultimately harmful to the client (nonmaleficence)?

SUGGESTION FOR FURTHER ROLE-PLAY IN CLASS

After each of the role-plays in this video, we recommend encouraging your students to enact their own role-plays based on the scenario they just saw in the video. Ask one of your students to become the client and play the part of hearing voices and being followed by others. Then, have several different students assume the role of therapist with this client. Each student can demonstrate a slightly different way of dealing with the ethical issues involved in this situation.

In general, for each of the role-plays that are enacted in this video, a standard list of questions might be usefully applied to each situation. Some of these questions are:

- How much guidance can you find by reviewing the ethics codes in thinking through the best ethical course for each case?
- Are there any legal issues involved in the case?
- What are the value issues in each case?
- If you were the counselor in each case, how might your values pertaining to this situation influence what you would say to the client or the actions you would take?
- If you had a value conflict with a client in each of these cases, how might you deal with the conflict?
- If you were to consult a colleague for each case, what might you want from this consultation? What questions would you ask? Where might you feel stuck?

COUNSELOR SELF-AWARENESS

A second section of Segment One of this program deals with a discussion of counselor self-awareness. Some of the questions that we encourage students to examine include: "What am I doing? Why am I doing it? What is in the best interests of my clients?" At this point you might want to raise the question of who is the best judge of the degree to which a client's interests are being considered.

Refer to some of the concluding ideas we make in *Issues and Ethics* (pp. 420–421). The fundamental question we pose that has implications for counselor self-awareness is: "Who has the right to counsel another person?"

Some questions to pose to students: "What makes you think that you can help anyone? What do you have to offer the people you are counseling? Are you doing in your own life what you encourage your clients to do?"

Another key point we make in the video is the importance of paying attention to yourself as a practitioner, rather than focusing on the ethics of others. It is a good idea to emphasize self-monitoring as a way to put the focus on our own actions.

Refer to *Issues and Ethics*, (Chapter 2, pp. 34–38) on the topic of self-awareness, personal needs of counselors, and unresolved personal issues.

Refer to *Becoming a Helper*, (Chapter 1, pp. 4–7) where we talk about needs of helpers. It is essential that students acquire awareness of their own needs and how these needs are likely to influence the interventions they make with clients. In *Becoming a Helper*, some of the needs we identify include:

- The need to make an impact
- The need to return a favor
- The need to care for others
- The need for self-help
- The need to be needed
- The need for money
- The need for prestige and status
- The need to provide answers
- The need for control

As you and your students watch the various role-plays, ask what needs seem to be evident in the therapists. Consider, for example, the therapist's (Nadine's) need to provide the client (John) with answers in the "Raising Kids" vignette (10:53).

QUESTIONS FOR CLASS DISCUSSION

- What are some ethical issues involved with a counselor's practice of giving abundant advice to John?
- What might you do with a client who begged you for advice?
- Are there certain situations where giving clients advice is justified? Should the cultural considerations be a factor in deciding if providing advice is appropriate?
- Some counselors have a need to give advice, thinking that if they can't offer advice, then they are not doing their job. If you refused to offer advice to clients, do you see other ways of assisting them in coming to their own answers?

After students view this role-play, have other students in your class role-play a client who actually wants advice from a counselor. Different students can role-play the therapist and show how they would deal with this situation.

SOME KEY POINTS FOR SELF-AWARENESS OF COUNSELOR

- It is essential that you become aware of your unresolved personal conflicts, if you hope to be able to be objective with clients and work effectively with them.
- The work of being a counselor will carry over into your personal life.
- Working with a client's deepest struggles are bound to open up some of your unfinished issues.
- Counselor training programs would do well to inform prospective students from the beginning of their program of the importance of participating in therapeutic experiences and seeking personal growth opportunities.

Refer to *Becoming a Helper*, pages 311–312, especially the section on the wounded healer.

Refer to *Issues and Ethics*, pages 38–44, on personal therapy for counselors and therapy during training.

Some questions to explore in class discussion:

- What are some reasons for strongly encouraging personal therapy for counseling students?
- Is ongoing therapy for practitioners an option? When should practitioners seek their own therapy?

- What is the responsibility of a counselor training program in the area of providing self-exploration opportunities for trainees?

MULTICULTURAL PERSPECTIVES

The third section of Segment One of this program deals with the multicultural dimensions of ethical practice. Part of being an ethical practitioner implies accounting for the cultural backgrounds of your clients. In making ethical decisions, you cannot leave the cultural context out of this process. It is essential to understand the role that cultural diversity plays in counseling practice.

In the role-play, "Seeking More from Life," (14:02) the client (Lucia) is presenting her struggle, which can be understood only to the extent that the counselor (Janice) understands her client's cultural values. In this case, Lucia is struggling with a decision of what she wants to do with her life. Her parents would like her to stay at home and take care of her children. She asks Janice how she might be able to help her.

We could easily have a counselor who imposes values and pushes the client to make decisions that are not congruent with the client's cultural values. However, the therapist lets the client (Lucia) know that she will listen to her and help her sort out her own values. The counselor lets Lucia know that the most important thing is that she is at peace with whatever decisions she makes.

This role-play can be used as a springboard for discussion of what it takes for a counselor to be able to ethically and effectively counsel diverse client populations. Focus especially on the characteristics of effective multicultural helpers, which are described in both *Becoming a Helper* (in Chapter 7) and *Issues and Ethics* (in Chapter 10).

A useful way to generate interaction among the students is to have them form small groups and share their reactions to the ethical issues illustrated by the role-play. After about 15 minutes, the entire class convenes and each group presents the highlights of their discussion. From here, it is often natural to ask for a few volunteers to demonstrate via role-play how they might approach the situation differently than what they just viewed in the video. Of course, after each role-play it is likely that the advantages and disadvantages of various actions will become apparent. It may be possible to devote close to an entire class session to viewing a single role-play scenario, discussing it, and having follow-up role-plays enacted in class.

KEY POINTS

- Strive to develop sensitivity to your clients' cultural values, yet do not burden yourself with needing to know everything about your client's culture.

Be sensitive enough to know that your clients may not see the world as you do.
- It is not realistic to expect that you will know everything about the cultural values of all of your clients. What is important is to enlist the help of your clients.
- Let your clients teach you what is essential to make the helping process effective. Put the focus on the clients and why they come to counseling.
- What if you as a counselor want to affirm the client's values?
- How might you help the client to clarify her own goals and options? How can you help the client explore her struggles, rather than provide her with solutions?
- What do the codes state about respecting diversity?

The ACA *Code of Ethics* provides the following standard on respecting differences:

> Counselors will actively attempt to understand the diverse cultural backgrounds of the clients with whom they work. This includes, but is not limited to, learning how the counselor's own cultural/ethnic/racial identity impacts her/his values and beliefs about the counseling process.

- How would you apply the above standard to any of the role plays enacted in the video?

REFERENCES

1. See *Issues and Ethics* (Chapter 10) on Multicultural Perspectives and Diversity Issues.
   - You might have students complete the self-inventory on pages 317–318. This inventory deals with attitudes pertaining to multicultural issues, especially from an ethical perspective.
   - Pay attention to the section on cultural tunnel vision on pages 320–323. If you are culturally encapsulated, how does this become an ethical issue?
   - Review the relevant ethical codes that pertain to multicultural counseling (pp. 324–325).
   - See the section dealing with multicultural training for counselors (pp. 338–343). Note especially the multicultural counseling competencies described on pages 340–341. Help your students to assess their current level of competency in the multicultural area.

2. Refer to *Becoming a Helper*, (Chapter 7, pp. 190–193) on addressing the importance of developing multicultural competencies. This section of the chapter will help your students to take an inventory of their current level of awareness, knowledge, and skills needed to work ethically and effectively with culturally diverse client populations.

OTHER REFERENCES

Herlihy, B., & Corey, G. (1996a). *ACA ethical standards casebook* (5th ed.). Alexandria, VA: American Counseling Association.

Refer to Chapter 2: Ethical Issues in Multicultural Counseling for a case study by Derald Wing Sue.

MULTICULTURAL COUNSELING COMPETENCIES: A SELF EXAMINATION

The self examination on the following pages will allow students to evaluate their current level of competence in dealing with multicultural issues in counseling. You may want to use it in conjunction with viewing the video segment on multicultural issues and as a basis for classroom discussion or small group work to identify areas for further work.

Multicultural Counseling Competencies: A Self Examination

The following is a self-examination on how well you are able to demonstrate multicultural counseling competencies based on standards proposed by Sue, Arrendondo, and McDavis (1992). It is for your own use in evaluating how well you are doing in becoming competent as a counselor of clients whose cultural background differs from yours.

This self-assessment is not intended as a research instrument and is certainly not intended to compete with other excellent research protocols.

Score yourself on a 5 point criteria giving yourself a grade for each question based on the following criteria.

A = always   B = often   C = sometimes   D = seldom   F = never

I. Counselor Awareness, Knowledge, and Skills

1. I actively work on becoming more aware of my own cultural heritage.
2. I constantly seek to become more aware of different cultural heritages.
3. I strive to understand and value cultural heritages that differ from my own.
4. I work at understanding how my own cultural background influences my beliefs, values, attitudes, and biases about psychological processes.
5. I regularly evaluate the limits of my competencies and expertise in counseling persons from different cultural backgrounds.
6. I question my comfortableness with differences that exist between me and my clients in regard to race, ethnicity, culture, and beliefs.
7. I strive to understand how my own racial and cultural heritage affects my personal and professional definitions and biases about what is normal and abnormal.
8. I seek to understand how oppression, racism, discrimination, and stereotyping affects me personally.
9. I regularly question how I may have benefited or been adversely affected directly or indirectly by individual, institutional, or cultural racism.
10. I diligently work at uncovering my own beliefs, attitudes, and feelings regarding racism.
11. I seek to gain greater knowledge about how I socially impact others.
12. I strive to become ever more knowledgeable about my communication style and how it may facilitate or hinder working with clients who are culturally different from me.
13. I regularly seek out educational, consultative, and training experiences that enrich my understanding of culturally different populations.

14. I constantly engage in the process of understanding myself as a racial and cultural being.
15. I actively strive to achieve a non-racist identity.

II. Understanding the Worldview of the Culturally Different Client

16. I work at becoming aware of my negative emotional reactions toward racial and ethnic groups that may prove detrimental to my clients.
17. I willingly and regularly contrast my own beliefs and attitudes with those of culturally different clients with whom I work in a way that is non-judgmental.
18. I question myself constantly about any stereotypes and preconceived notions I hold toward other racial and ethnic minority groups.
19. I study to obtain specific knowledge and information about particular culturally different groups before trying to work with them individually or collectively.
20. I work to more thoroughly incorporate competencies that will help me in understanding the literature on minority identity developmental models.
21. I update myself regularly (at least every three months) in understanding how race, culture, and ethnicity may affect personality formation, vocational choices, manifestations of psychological disorders, help-seeking behavior, and the appropriateness of counseling approaches.
22. I actively engage in processes (such as reading, supervision, and discussions) that help me gain a greater awareness of how sociopolitical influences impinge upon the life of racial and ethnic minorities.
23. I interact with people of different cultures in striving to understand how immigration issues, poverty, racism, stereotyping, and powerlessness all leave major scars that may influence the counseling process.
24. I familiarize myself as often as possible (but at least quarterly) with relevant and up-to-date research regarding the mental health and disorders of various ethnic and racial groups.
25. I actively seek out educational experiences that enrich my knowledge, understanding, and cross-cultural skills.
26. I am actively involved with individuals, outside of counseling settings, whose cultural heritage differs from mine in order to more fully appreciate and understand their lives and life styles.

III. Developing Appropriate Intervention Strategies and Techniques

27. I seek to recognize as well as respect my clients' religious and spiritual beliefs and values about physical and mental functioning.
28. I strive to understand and respect indigenous helping practices and minority community intrinsic help-giving networks.

29. I value and appreciate bilingualism.
30. I do not view another language as an impediment to counseling.
31. I seek to know and understand how generic characteristics of counseling (e.g., culture or class bound) may clash with cultural values of various minority groups.
32. I strive to recognize institutional barriers that prevent minorities from using mental health services.
33. I examine potential bias in assessment instruments on a regular basis.
34. I use assessment procedures and interpret assessment findings in regard to the cultural and linguistic characteristics of my clients.
35. I regularly study about minority family structures, hierarchies, values, and beliefs.
36. I seek out knowledge about the community characteristics and resources where I live.
37. I make it my business to become aware of relevant discriminatory practices at the social and community level that may be affecting the psychological welfare of my clients and minority culture populations.
38. I work constantly at becoming skilled and able to engage in a variety of verbal and nonverbal helping responses, including the accurate and appropriate sending and receiving of verbal and nonverbal messages.
39. I resist becoming tied down to any one method or approach to helping.
40. When I sense that my helping style is limited and potentially inappropriate, I work at anticipating and ameliorating its negative impact.
41. I question myself periodically as to when I should exercise institutional intervention skills on behalf of clients.
42. I focus with clients to help them determine whether a problem stems from racism or bias in others so that they do not inappropriately blame themselves.
43. I seek consultation from traditional healers or religious and spiritual leaders and practitioners when it is appropriate in the treatment of culturally different clients.
44. I take responsibility for interacting in the language requested by my clients even if it means making a referral to outside resources, such as a bilingual counselor, or finding a translator with cultural knowledge and an appropriate professional background.
45. I regularly engage in training and becoming more of an expert in the use of traditional assessment and testing instruments and in understanding their technical aspects as well as cultural limitations.
46. I work toward eliminating biases, prejudices, and discriminatory practices.
47. I strive to become increasingly cognizant of the sociopolitical contexts in conducting evaluations and providing interventions.

48. I sensitize myself through various means to issues of oppression, sexism, and racism.
49. I take responsibility in educating my clients about the processes of psychological intervention, such as goals, expectations, legal rights, and my counseling orientation.

Scores on this self-administered instrument range from "A" to "F." There are three areas in which to assess yourself:

1) Counselor Attitude, Knowledge, and Skills, Items 1–15   My Grade _____
2) Understanding the Worldview of the Culturally Different Client, Items 16–26   My Grade _____
3) Developing Appropriate Intervention Strategies and Techniques, Items 27–49   My Grade _____

My Total Grade _____

Since all of the above three areas are related, a low grade in any one will impact the other two. Therefore, in evaluating your score, you should look at both your area grades as well as your total grade. Ways to constructively improve your grades include:

- examining your own cultural heritage and background,
- attending workshops and classes on multicultural counseling,
- obtaining supervision from a skilled multicultural counselor,
- reading books and journal articles,
- joining a group that studies multicultural issues,
- viewing videos on multicultural counseling,
- participating in interactive computer software focused on multicultural counseling,
- becoming a member of a professional group that deals with multicultural counseling issues, such as the Association for Multicultural Counseling and Development,
- participating in minority culture events in your community, and working in the sociopolitical arena to bring about needed changes.

Source: Adapted from S. T. Gladding, P. Pedersen, and D. Stone, "Multicultural Counseling Competencies: A Self Examination," *ACES Spectrum Newsletter,* Winter, 1997, Vol. 58, No. 2. Reprinted with permission of authors.

SEGMENT TWO: VALUES AND THE HELPING RELATIONSHIP

KEY POINTS IN SEGMENT TWO

- Many clients come to counseling because they are sorting out their values. Counselors often have strong values in certain areas, but it is important that they do not impose their values on clients.
- Counselors may not agree with some of the values of their clients, yet it is essential that they respect the rights of clients to hold a different set of values.
- As counselors, you will certainly have your values, but hopefully you will not push them onto your clients. Instead, it is the counselor's role to help clients clarify their own values and make their own decisions based on their values.
- The role of informed consent regarding how values may influence the counseling process is particulary important. If you have definite values in certain areas that will likely influence your work with clients, they have a right to know this from the outset.
- From an ethical perspective, counseling ethically implies that, as counselors, you are aware of your personal values. The *Code of Ethics* of ACA states: "Counselors are aware of their own values, attitudes, beliefs, and behaviors and how they apply in a diverse society, and avoid imposing their values on clients."
- As a counselor, even if you do not aim to impose your values on your clients, you may unintentionally influence them in subtle ways to embrace your values. Because your clients tend to want your approval, they are likely to pick up subtle messages from you and decide and act in ways that they imagine will meet with your favor, rather than developing their own inner direction.

SOME KEY QUESTIONS TO POSE TO STUDENTS ON ETHICS AND VALUES

1. Impact of counselor's values
   - Is it best not to reveal your values to your clients, lest you bias the direction clients are likely to take?
   - As counselors, how can you become increasingly aware of the impact of your values on your clients?
   - Can and should you keep your values out of the counseling process?

- If you have definite values that you think clients should adopt, does ethical practice imply that you make these values known to potential clients through the informed consent process?
- To what degree are you open to having your own values challenged?

2. Exposing values versus imposing values
   - What is the difference between exposing and imposing one's values?
   - What are the ethical issues in persuasion and power?
   - Is it ever appropriate to impose values on clients—and is it ever effective?
   - What are the ethical issues involved in pushing your values on clients?

3. Teaching of values in counseling
   - What are some values and assumptions that are an integral part of the counseling process?
   - Should clients be told about the implications of such value orientations that are a basic aspect of the counseling relationship?
   - Is the purpose of counseling to teach values to clients or to teach clients how to discover their own values?
   - How can your values impact counseling for better or for worse?

4. Values clarification
   - How can you clarify your values and understand their effects on your work?
   - What are some ways that you can help clients clarify their values?
   - If clients are uncertain, is it your job to provide clients with a direction?
   - What are some ways to increase the chances that clients will engage in a struggle and find their own answers?
   - If clients ask you for direction, advice, or for answers, what is the best course of action to take?

5. Value conflicts
   - How can situations be dealt with when a conflict exists between your values and a client's?
   - What are some struggles you experience as a result of value differences between you and your clients?
   - What is your responsibility in examining how certain values of yours may interfere with counseling?
   - When is consultation an appropriate course of action?
   - What are some concerns that you experience pertaining to the impact of your values in your work?

- When might you find it necessary to refer clients because of value differences between the two of you?

REFERENCES

1. See *Issues and Ethics*, Chapter 3, especially the discussion on inventory of your values as a counselor (pp. 67–68), clarifying your values (pp. 68–71), ethics of imposing your values on clients (pp. 71–72). There are several inventories that you can have your students take (such as the one on pages 67–68 and the one on value conflicts on pages 72–73).
2. Refer to *Becoming a Helper*, Chapter 6, on the role of values, imposing versus exposing values, value conflicts with clients. Page 154 offers focus questions, some of which you can pose to your students at this juncture. If you are interested in an inventory that students can complete, have them take the inventory on pages 155–156.

DISCUSSION WITH STUDENTS ON VALUES

In the video, several students comment on how they expect their values might influence their counseling practice. For instance, one student would have trouble with clients who hold racist beliefs. Another student would have trouble with clients who hold fundamentalist religious beliefs. Ask your students to identify areas where they might expect to have difficulty because of a conflict between their values and the values of certain clients.

RELIGION/SPIRITUALITY

This role-play, "Religion as Answer," (20:55) portrays a conflict of values between the client and the counselor. The client, LeAnne, thinks that prayer should be her answer to her personal problems. She thinks that she is not hearing the Lord clearly. Her counselor, Suzanne, has some trouble in understanding what her client's religion means to her or to work with LeAnne's religious framework within the context of counseling. Instead, Suzanne comments that she feels that she is in competition with God and the client's religion. She wants her to put more faith in the counseling process as an answer to her problems.

QUESTIONS FOR CLASS DISCUSSION

- If you were the client in this situation, how might you have felt? To what degree did you feel heard? Do you think you would have wanted to come back to the counselor?
- How might the counselor's values or personal experiences with religion have potentially hindered the effective exploration of LeAnne's struggles within the context of her religious framework?

- Is it ethical to challenge the client's belief in the power of prayer and her reliance on God to solve her problems? As her counselor, if you thought she was avoiding personal responsibility by relying on reading Scripture and praying, what might you say to her? Would you ask her if she is having trouble in relying on her religion?
- Do you think it is possible to incorporate religious values into counseling, even if the client may be unwilling to examine her motivations for praying?
- Is it appropriate to deal with religious issues in an open and forthright manner as clients' needs arise in the therapy process?
- Do clients have the right to explore their religious concerns in counseling?
- Are counselors forcing their values on their clients if they are not willing to explore religious themes when clients introduce them in a therapy session?
- What role does spirituality or religion play in your life? Does it provide you with a source of meaning?
- What have been some of your life experiences pertaining to religion and spirituality? How might your own experiences either help or hinder you in being objective with your clients?
- As a counselor, how do you think that your spiritual/religious beliefs will influence your ability to be present for your client when they struggle with these concerns?

KEY POINTS

- Counselors are being challenged to incorporate spiritual and religious beliefs in both assessment and treatment practices.
- Exploring spiritual and religious values with clients may help them find solutions to their problems.
- It is essential that counselors remain open and nonjudgmental in listening to clients who want to discuss their spiritual beliefs.
- What is important is that counselors understand and respect the client's religious and spiritual beliefs and include such beliefs in the assessment and treatment process.

REFERENCES

1. See *Becoming a Helper*, (Chapter 6, pp. 166–170) on Values and the Helping Relationship for a discussion of religious and spiritual values. Several situations are presented, along with questions to help students clarify their stance on given issues. For example, on page 167 a client

named Peter has a strong fundamentalist background. He has clear ideas about right and wrong, sin, guilt, and damnation, and he has accepted the teachings of his church without question. This different, but related case, could be role-played in class as a way to explore a variety of other issues related to counseling a client with a religious background.
2. See *Issues and Ethics*, (Chapter 3, pp. 82–90) on Values and the Helping Relationship, for a treatment of the role of spiritual and religious values in counseling. There are a variety of cases that can easily be role-played in class. This section contains a discussion of the ethical issues involved in the assessment and treatment of spiritual and religious values.

VALUE CONFLICT

This role-play, "Abortion," (24:36) represents a value clash between client and counselor. The client (Sally) is considering an abortion and the therapist has difficulty with this possible decision. Lucia, the counselor, says that she is feeling uncomfortable because of her belief that life begins at conception. Lucia tells Sally that she will have to get some consultation so that she can sort out her thinking.

QUESTIONS FOR CLASS DISCUSSION

- If you were the client in this situation, how might you have felt? Do you think you would have wanted to come back to the counselor?
- If you were Sally's counselor, how might you respond to her?
- Was Lucia's disclosure that she had trouble with Sally's possible abortion helpful to the client? Might this have burdened the client with one more variable?
- Lucia stated that she wanted her client to consider her options objectively and make the best decision for herself. Do you think it would be likely that Sally would be able to do this, knowing what her counselor thinks about abortion? Do you think her counselor is capable of assisting Sally in making her own decision in this case?
- What basic moral principles need to be considered in analyzing this situation? (Autonomy; nonmaleficence; beneficence; justice; fidelity; veracity) For example, how does autonomy apply, or this client's right to self-determination? What about beneficence? What is best for this client? How about veracity? (What promises did the counselor make to the client?)

After students have role-played the above vignette, it may be useful to provide another scenario that students will role-play and use as a springboard for discussion. For example, consider reframing the scenario that was illustrated in the video in this way. Sally tells you as her counselor: "I just found out I am pregnant. I am really not ready to have a child and I'm not sure what to do. I don't want to give my child up for adoption. And I'm not sure that I am open to having an abortion. My religious values and moral convictions would make it extremely difficult to choose abortion. Really, I can see no option, yet I know I must make some choice. Can you help me?"

Students can enact the above role-play and show how they would deal with the religious and moral values of the client. What kinds of help might they provide to this client who is struggling to find a resolution that she'll be able to live with?

With the modifications of this case described above, consider these questions:

- Would you be inclined to suggest a solution to your client? If so, what kind of suggestion might you offer?
- Would you counsel Sally differently knowing that she is personally opposed to abortion because of her religious values?
- How might you help her find her own answers within her?
- How do you think that your own religious and moral values could influence the interventions you make in this situation?
- Would the age of the client make a difference? How about her cultural background?

KEY POINTS

- It is not the counselor's role to make a decision for the client in her struggle to decide what to do in this case.
- A counselor is not working for the client's best interest if he or she either pushes Sally to have an abortion or instills guilt in her as a way to prevent her from having an abortion.
- Consultation would be helpful for a counselor who admits to having a bias that would interfere with allowing the client to make her own choice in this matter.
- The counselor should consider referring the client to another counselor when a value conflict makes it difficult to work effectively and objectively with the client.

REFERENCES

1. See *Becoming a Helper*, (Chapter 6, pp. 170–171) on Values and the Helping Relationship, for a case pertaining to abortion, which is followed by guides for discussion.
2. See *Issues and Ethics*, (Chapter 3, pp. 73–75) on Values and the Helping Relationship, for the case of Candy, which also illustrates ethical issues in dealing with a pregnant minor.

SEXUAL ORIENTATION

In this role-play, "Coming Out," (27:00) the client (Conrad) brings out his homosexual orientation. Conrad states that this is something that he is struggling with, mainly because it is not accepted in his culture or in his religion. The client admits that he trusts his counselor (John) and it feels good to be able to make this disclosure. Conrad wants his counselor's help in coming out to his friends and family. So, it appears that the client wants to explore his thoughts and feelings about his sexual orientation in light of his cultural and religious values.

Conrad finds the counselor being unreceptive at best. John, the counselor, says, "Are you sure this is the best thing for you?" Then John discloses that he does not approve of "the homosexual life-style" and adds that he does not see it as "being very healthy." Conrad has negative reactions to John's judgmental attitude and lack of acceptance of who he is as a person.

QUESTIONS FOR CLASS DISCUSSION

- What are the ethical issues in this vignette?
- If you were the client in this case, how do you imagine you'd feel after hearing from your counselor that he does not approve of homosexuality?
- Does John's self-disclosure about his view of homosexuality help or hinder Conrad (client)? Is this disclosure a burden to the client? How appropriate is it? How can a counselor determine when and how much to disclose in value-laden areas? Would it have been better for John to discuss his views with his supervisor before he shared them with Conrad?
- If a counselor is not able to support a client's sexual orientation, should a referral be made? Should the counselor seek consultation? Do you think this counselor should engage in his own work to determine why he would feel a need to change his client?
- What if the client doesn't disclose his or her sexual orientation until months after the beginning of a counseling relationship. If you did not approve of gay/lesbian relationships, what would you do if this became an issue later in the counseling relationship?

- What basic moral principles need to be considered in analyzing this situation? (Autonomy; nonmaleficence; beneficence; justice; fidelity; veracity)
- The ethical codes of the ACA, the APA, and the NASW clearly state that discrimination on the basis of race, ethnicity, gender, or sexual orientation is unethical and unacceptable. In light of this guideline, what are the implications for practitioners who claim that they could not work with a gay or lesbian client because they are morally opposed to this sexual orientation?

KEY POINTS

- As a counselor, you may need to seek supervision or consultation.
- It is essential that you be able to work with clients without your values getting in the way. It is important for you to put aside your biases so that you are in a position to hear what your client is presenting to you.
- Your client needs a nonjudgmental atmosphere. No client will open up if he or she feels judged. Even exposing values on the counselor's part can be a problem to the client.
- In this case, the challenge is to work with the client in such a manner that you could assist him in making decisions that are congruent with his own value system.

REFERENCES

1. See *Becoming a Helper*, (Chapter 6, pp. 160–163) on Values and the Helping Relationship, for a case situation pertaining to gay and lesbian issues, which is followed by guides for discussion and a commentary.
2. See *Issues and Ethics*, (Chapter 3, pp. 99–106) on Values and the Helping Relationship, for a treatment of ethical and value issues in counseling gay and lesbian clients.

END-OF-LIFE DECISIONS

In this role-play, "Talk of Suicide," (31:32) the client (Gary) is HIV positive and is seriously considering suicide.

The counselor (Natalie) tells Gary that she can't believe what she is hearing from Gary. The counselor is doing her best to persuade him not to take his life. She tells him that he is taking the easy way out by choosing to end his life. She asks him if he has a plan. She asks him to think about his family and other options. She lets him know that he may be in a crisis state and not able to make a good decision. Is imposition of a counselor's values in this case justified?

The counselor can have a definite agenda for her client. She doesn't want her client to take his life. She wants him to explore other options. She is concerned about Gary's welfare and the welfare of his family. This vignette raises both ethical and legal issues including those of confidentiality and the duty to warn.

QUESTIONS FOR CLASS DISCUSSION

- What are the ethical issues involved in this role-play?
- What are the legal issues involved?
- Are you aware of the laws of your state and the ethical guidelines of your professional organization concerning an individual's freedom to make end-of-life decisions?
- Do you see any potential conflict between the ethical and legal issues in this situation?
- What are the confidentiality issues with both HIV positive and suicidal clients?
- What are your values with respect to the right to die?
- Where do you stand with respect to key questions on end-of-life decisions? What is your position on an individual's right to decide about matters pertaining to living and dying?
- What religious, ethical, and moral beliefs do you hold that might enable you to support Gary's decision about ending his life due to the circumstances of the case?
- How might your beliefs get in the way of assisting Gary in making his own decision?
- If Gary were your client, would you respect his self-determination, or would you influence him to search for alternatives to suicide at this stage in his life?
- Do you have the responsibility and the right to forcefully protect Gary from the potential harm his own decisions may bring—to both himself and his family?
- Do you have an ethical right to block Gary if he insists that he wants to choose death over life? Do you have an ethical duty to respect Gary's decision, assuming that he thinks this issue through thoroughly?
- Do you think that imposing your values (of staying alive) might be justified in this case?
- If there were no legal mandates to report Gary's intentions "to do himself in," would you feel justified (as did Natalie) in attempting to persuade Gary to accept the priority you place on life?

- If Gary were your client, would you ask if he had a plan to kill himself? If he did have a plan, what might you do? If he said that he just began thinking about this and doesn't have a plan, but wants to talk with you about how he might end his life, what would you be inclined to say or do?
- Because Gary is rational and able to make decisions that affect his life, should he be allowed to take measures to end his life long before he becomes terminally ill?
- Because Gary is not yet seriously ill, should he be prevented from ending his life, even if it means taking away his freedom of choice?
- What basic moral principles need to be considered in analyzing the issues in this case? (Autonomy; nonmaleficence; beneficence; justice; fidelity; veracity)

KEY POINTS

- As a counselor, you need to be able to discuss end-of-life decisions with clients when they bring these concerns to you.
- If you are not willing to examine your own values and beliefs in this area, it is likely that you'll not be able to encourage your clients to explore their values and make their own decisions. You may interrupt dialogues with clients, cut off an exploration of their feelings about such issues, or provide clients with your answers, instead of assisting them to find their own answers.
- In cases such as this, consultation is of the utmost importance.
- Along with consultation, it is also essential to keep good records and document discussions with your client and actions you took to prevent the client from harming himself or herself.

REFERENCES

1. See *Issues and Ethics* (Chapter 3, pp. 90–97) on the section of end-of-life decisions.
   - Review the National Association of Social Worker's policy statement on end-of-life decisions (pp. 93–94). You could use this policy statement as a framework for discussing the issues involved in Gary's case.
   - After students have had a chance to discuss this role-play, and have also done several role-plays in class with this vignette, have them read the cases in the textbook on pages 91–97.

- Review the case of Andrew (p. 91). [This case is much like the case of Gary. See the discussion on "Suicide: A free and rational choice?" (pp. 92–93). Gary's and Andrew's cases can be applied to this discussion.]
- Review the discussion on the topic of potential conflicts between law and ethics (pp. 94–96). Discuss the case of Festus (pp. 95–96) that illustrates how legal and ethical issues can be in conflict.
- See the case of Emily (p. 96) and the case of Bettina (p. 97), both of which raise issues involved in end-of-life decisions.

2. See *Becoming a Helper* (Chapter 5, pp. 128–130) on the section dealing with the counselor's obligation to warn and protect.
  - Under the harm-to-self section, the point is made of considering both ethical and legal issues in a case illustrated by the role-play with Gary and Natalie. "Many therapists inform their clients that they have an ethical and legal responsibility to break confidentiality when they have good reason to suspect suicidal behavior. Even if clients take the position that they are free to do with their lives what they want, therapists have a legal duty to protect them. The problem is to determine when a client is serious about committing suicide" (p. 129).

SUGGESTIONS FOR ROLE-PLAYING

With all of the above cases, students can enact them in class. It is always a good idea to first set up a role-play situation, perhaps having more than one therapist, so that several approaches can be demonstrated and discussed. The discussion following the role-play will be a lot more lively and concrete once the scenario is enacted.

OTHER REFERENCES

Herlihy, B., & Corey, G. (1996a). *ACA ethical standards casebook* (5th ed.). Alexandria, VA: American Counseling Association.

Refer to Chapter 10, The Relationship between Law and Ethics, for a case study by Theodore P. Remley. Also refer to Chapter 8, Working with Suicidal Clients, for a case study of counseling a suicidal teenager by Robert E. Wubbolding.

SEGMENT THREE: BOUNDARY ISSUES AND MULTIPLE RELATIONSHIPS

In our opening comments on boundary issues and multiple relationships, we attempt to highlight a few key points that apply to managing boundaries and multiple relationships.

KEY POINTS IN SEGMENT THREE

- What do the ethics codes say about multiple relationships? They are not strictly prohibited. In fact, some are unavoidable. However, it may be prudent not to become involved in avoidable dual or multiple relationships.
- The main point is that clients must not be harmed or exploited if multiple relationships exist. The key element is abuse of power on the therapist's part, not simply multiple relating.
- Remain focused on the consequences to the client of getting involved in a multiple relationship.
- What makes dual or multiple relationships so problematic? Herlihy and Corey (1997a) emphasize that dual or multiple relationships are rarely a clear-cut matter. The task facing practitioners is to make judgment calls and to apply codes of ethics carefully to specific situations (many of which were enacted in this part of the video program). The reasons dual or multiple relationships are problematic are that:
    (1) they can be difficult to recognize;
    (2) they can be very harmful, but they are not always harmful;
    (3) they are the subject of conflicting views; and
    (4) they are not always avoidable.

REFERENCES

1. See *Issues and Ethics* (p. 227) for a summary of all the codes. On pages 224–225 is a self-inventory for students to assess beliefs and practices pertaining to managing boundaries and multiple relationships. A good way to begin a consideration of this topic is to assist students in taking a self-inventory to identify their positions on the topics that will be addressed in the video.
2. In *Issues and Ethics* see also the discussion in the section on Dual and Multiple Relationships in Perspective (pp. 226–231). What are the different perspectives on these issues?
3. See *Issues and Ethics* (pp. 228–231) on Designing Safeguards to Protect Clients.
4. See also the discussion in *Becoming a Helper* (pp. 131–134) on Keeping Relationships with Clients Professional: The Dual Relationship Controversy.

OTHER REFERENCES

(See the References section at the end of this Facilitator's Resource Manual.)

In preparing for your class on the topic of boundary issues and multiple relationships, you may want to consult other sources besides *Issues and Ethics* and *Becoming a Helper*. We suggest: Herlihy, B., & Corey, G. (1997a). *Boundary issues in counseling: Multiple roles and responsibilities.* Alexandria, VA: American Counseling Association. In this book, the following sections are of particular relevance to the topic explored in the first part of the third segment of this video dealing with boundary issues:

- Chapter 1—Boundary Issues in Perspective
- Chapter 11—Key Themes, Questions, and Decision Making

In the final chapter of their book, *Boundary Issues in Counseling: Multiple Roles and Relationships*, Herlihy and Corey (1997) discuss ten themes that provide the following guidelines for practitioners in dealing with multiple relationships.

1. Multiple relationship issues affect virtually all mental health practitioners, regardless of their work setting or clientele.
2. All professional codes of ethics caution against dual relationships, but the newer codes acknowledge the complex nature of these relationships.
3. Not all multiple relationships can be avoided, nor are they necessarily always harmful.
4. Multiple role relationships challenge us to monitor ourselves and to examine the motivations for our practices.
5. Whenever we consider becoming involved in a dual or multiple relationship, we would be wise to seek consultation from trusted colleagues or a supervisor.
6. There are few absolute answers that can neatly resolve dual or multiple relationship dilemmas.
7. The intenton for entering into dual or multiple relationships should be for the benefit of our clients or others served rather than to protect ourselves from censure.
8. In determining whether to proceed with a dual or multiple relationship, consider whether the potential benefit of the relationship outweighs the potential for harm.
9. It is the responsibility of counselor preparation programs to introduce boundary issues and explore multiple relationship questions. It is important to teach students ways of thinking about alternative courses of action.
10. Counselor education programs have a responsibility to develop their own guidelines, policies, and procedures for dealing with multiple roles and role conflicts within the program.

Herlihy, B., & Corey, G. (1996a). *ACA ethical standards casebook* (5th ed.). Alexandria, VA: American Counseling Association.

Refer to Chapter 7: Dual Relationships, which includes a case study by Holly Forester-Miller.

QUESTIONS FOR CLASS DISCUSSION

- Are multiple relationships necessarily unethical and unprofessional?
- What do the ethics codes of the various professional organizations state regarding dual or multiple relationships?
- What makes dual or multiple relationships so problematic?
- What is the difference between avoidable multiple relationships and unavoidable multiple relationships?
- What are some ways to create safeguards if multiple relationships are unavoidable?
- Do you think that social relationships with current clients are ever appropriate or ethical? What about with former clients?
- When, if ever, would you consider developing a social relationship with a former client?
- Under what conditions, if ever, might you consider attending a special event of a client, such as a wedding reception or a graduation party?
- If you were sexually attracted to a client, how do you expect that you would deal with this situation?
- How might you deal with a situation in which a client discloses his or her sexual attraction to you?
- Under what conditions, if ever, might you consider bartering arrangements with a client?
- How do cultural considerations play into the deliberation of bartering?
- Under what conditions, if ever, might you consider accepting a gift from a client?
- What cultural considerations might influence your decision to accept a gift?
- What cultural issues might you consider in establishing and maintaining boundaries in counseling relationships?

SUGGESTIONS FOR ROLE-PLAYS

All of the above questions can be explored through the medium of role-play. In our classes, we frequently create a brief scenario and ask for volunteers to become the therapist. Oftentimes we act as the client so that we can set up the situation through dramatization. We generally like to get several students to try their hand at dealing with a given situation so that everyone in class can see more than one way of dealing with a potentially problematic case. The textbooks contain a number of cases that can be role-played in addition to the ones that are presented in this program. Of course, in the Student Version of the *Ethics in Action* video, there are a number of other role-plays on the areas below that can be enacted and discussed in class.

SOCIAL RELATIONSHIPS

This role-play, "The Wedding," (38:43) illustrates a case of client (Richard) who wants his counselor (Suzanne) to come to his wedding and reception. He stresses that it would mean a lot to him if she attended both his wedding and the reception afterward. Suzanne is uncomfortable in granting the client his request of going to the reception, but agrees to attend the marriage ceremony.

In the discussion following this role-play, a number of points are made in the discussion.

- It's important to Richard that his therapist participate in this special day for him.
- He'd be offended if she did not attend. There is a cultural issue involved for Richard.
- In the discussion, a student says that she would understand the Latino culture and would see it as an opportunity to learn more about her client by attending these events.
- If the counselor were to go to the reception, the counselor would have to deal with others who knew the client. What might she say to a person who asked, "How do you know Richard? Are you a friend of his?"

KEY POINTS

- This is a complex issue, not to be resolved with a simple answer.
- Some counselors will decide they do not want to get involved with clients in any way outside of the office. In many cases, it will depend upon the client and his or her ability to handle the dual or multiple relationship.
- It is crucial to assess how a social relationship is likely to impact the therapeutic relationship, or how meeting in a setting outside of the office may influence the professional relationship.
- Therapists need to be aware of their own needs and motivations and never place them above the needs of clients.
- The welfare of the client is always the primary consideration.
- Decisions should not be made on the basis of wanting to win the approval of the client.
- It is important to take into consideration the cultural dimensions of meeting outside the office.

REFERENCES

1. See *Issues and Ethics* (pp. 238–241) on the section, Social Relationships with Clients. The key question is: Do social relationships with clients necessarily interfere with therapeutic relationships?
2. In *Issues and Ethics* an additional case on page 240 addresses the case of a counseling intern. This is a good one to role-play in class.
3. See also the discussion on Combining Professional and Personal Relationships on pages 135–136 in *Becoming a Helper*—especially the section on Becoming Friends with Former Clients.

OTHER REFERENCES

(See the References section at the end of this Facilitator's Resource Manual.)

In preparing for your class on the topic of boundary issues and multiple relationships, you may want to consult other sources besides *Issues and Ethics* and *Becoming a Helper*. We suggest Herlihy, B., & Corey, G. (1997a). *Boundary issues in counseling: Multiple roles and responsibilities*. Alexandria, VA: American Counseling Association. In this book, the following sections are of particular relevance to the topic explored in the video:

- Counseling a Friend or Acquaintance (pp. 97–98).
- Social Relationships with Current Clients (pp. 102–103).
- Social Relationships with Former Clients (pp. 103–104).

SEXUAL ATTRACTION

In this role-play, "Client's Attraction," (43:25) the client (Gary) discloses his attraction to his counselor (LeAnne). The counselor attempts to deal with his attractions therapeutically by focusing on how his attraction might be a theme in his life and how it is related to some of the issues he has pursued in counseling, especially his relationship with women. While not wanting to minimize the client's attraction, the therapist does not want to feed her own ego.

The crux of the issue is how to deal with the attraction of the client to the therapist in an ethical and effective manner. The client had his own agenda and wanted to get his feelings out. He really didn't want to hear some of the things that his counselor was saying.

QUESTIONS FOR CLASS DISCUSSION

- What guidelines can you think of for dealing with sexual attractions in therapy in an ethical manner?

- If you were attracted to a client, would you ever reveal this to your client? Why or why not?
- How prepared do you feel to deal with attractions clients may have and express to you?

REFERENCES

1. See *Issues and Ethics* in Chapter 7 on Sexual Attractions in the Client-Therapist Relationship (pp. 241–245).
2. See *Issues and Ethics* (p. 243) for some suggestions on how counselors can deal with powerful attractions to clients.
3. See the case of Diana in *Issues and Ethics* (pp. 244–245) for another case to role-play in class.
4. See *Becoming a Helper* on pages 138–141. Here is a good list of behaviors to watch for as indicators of exceeding appropriate therapeutic boundaries. Also see the recommendations for strategies for managing attractions to clients.

OTHER REFERENCES

(See the References section at the end of this Facilitator's Resource Manual.)

Gill-Wigal and Heaton (1996), in their article, "Managing Sexual Attraction in the Therapeutic Relationship," offer some useful suggestions to practitioners for dealing ethically and effectively with sexual attractions.

- Never act out feelings of attraction. Avoid actions that could foster the attraction, such as sitting close to or hugging the client.
- Acknowledge (to yourself) feelings of attraction.
- Seek to understand these feelings through discussions with supervisors, colleagues, and personal therapists.
- Take responsibility for your feelings. Be alert to factors such as work stress and tendencies to rationalize or make the client responsible for the attraction.
- Monitor boundaries by setting clear limits on physical contact, self-disclosure, and client requests for personal information.
- Seek help.

BARTERING

In this role-play, "Manicuring for Therapy," (47:02) the client can no longer afford to pay the therapist. The client runs out of money and does not like to think about terminating. The therapist very quickly suggests bartering manicures and haircuts for therapy.

When a client is unable to afford therapy, or to continue therapy, he or she may offer a bartering arrangement. Most helpers go into the helping professions because they want to help. When clients are in a position where they are unable to pay, this taps into a profound issue.

QUESTIONS FOR CLASS DISCUSSION

- Would you ever initiate the possibility of bartering if a client informed you that he or she is unable to pay for therapy?
- What considerations would you examine in deciding whether or not to engage in bartering?
- What other options besides bartering might exist for a client who is unable to pay for therapy?

Students may think that bartering is a simply an unacceptable practice. Reviewing the ethical codes, they may see more potential problems in bartering than potential benefits. Some students may not consider, however, the cultural dimensions involved in bartering. See Holly Forester-Miller's (1997) article, "Rural Communities: Can Dual Relationships Be Avoided?" She writes: "Bartering is common practice in some regions and offers an opportunity for some individuals to receive counseling services. In the Appalachian culture, for example, it is a matter of pride to be able to provide for yourself and your loved ones." (p. 99)

REFERENCES

1. See *Issues and Ethics* on Bartering for Professional Services (pp. 234-238).

    What are the ethical standards on bartering? See page 235 for a summary of the different profession's codes pertaining to bartering. In general, these codes suggest that practitioners refrain from accepting goods or services from clients in return for counseling services because such arrangements have the potential for conflicts, exploitation, and distortion of the relationship.

    The ACA's code dealing with bartering reads as follows:

    > Counselors ordinarily refrain from accepting goods or services from clients in return for counseling services because such arrangements create inherent potential for conflicts, exploitation, and distortion of the professional relationship. Counselors may participate in bartering only if the relationship is not exploitive, if the client requests it, if a clear written contract is established, and if such arrangements are accepted practice among professionals in the community.

As can be seen from the code on bartering, generally, practitioners may participate in bartering only if the relationship is not exploitive, if the client requests it, if a clear written contract is established, and if such arrangements are accepted practice among professionals in the community.

There are a couple of extra cases in the text that lend themselves to role-playing. See the cases of Barbara and Olive in the text on page 237. As the instructor, you might want to engage in role-play—either as the client or at times, as the therapist.

2. See the section in *Becoming a Helper* on Bartering (pp. 136–138). Some other cases are described here that you might want to introduce for class practice and discussion.

OTHER REFERENCES

Herlihy, B., & Corey, G. (1997a). *Boundary issues in counseling: Multiple roles and responsibilities.* Alexandria, VA: American Counseling Association.

In this book, the following sections are of particular relevance to the topic explored in the video:

- Bartering for Goods or Services (pp. 96–97).
- Sue, D. W.__Multicultural Perspectives on Multiple Relationships (pp. 106–109).
- Forester-Miller, H.__Rural Communities: Can Dual Relationships Be Avoided? (pp. 99–100)

GIFT-GIVING

In this role-play, "The Vase," (50:16) the client (Sally) is grateful for the help from her counselor (Charlae) and wants to give her a vase. The client informs the therapist that giving gifts is a part of the Chinese culture. Charlae discusses her dilemma with wanting to accept the gift, but also the fact that the codes discourage her from accepting gifts from clients. The client lets her counselor know that she will feel rejected if this gift is not accepted.

QUESTIONS FOR CLASS DISCUSSION

- If you were the counselor in this situation, would you accept the vase? Why or why not?
- If the client informed you that by giving you a gift she would hope that a closer relationship would develop between you, how might you deal with this?

- If giving gifts were not a part of the client's culture, would you be inclined to accept an inexpensive gift? Why or why not?

KEY POINTS

Students may think that accepting a gift is a simple matter. Some may merely tell a client that they will not accept a gift because doing so might be viewed as unprofessional. In fact, at a workshop on law and ethics that we attended recently, the presenter cautioned against accepting gifts. The advice given was that if gifts are accepted for clinical or cultural reasons, then this should be documented.

However, from a multicultural perspective, gift-giving may be a common practice in some cultures—as was demonstrated in the role-play in this video. Sally wanted to offer her counselor a vase, which was inexpensive, as a sign of her appreciation. If the counselor refuses to accept this gift, might this damage the therapeutic relationship or reverse some of the gains made in the counseling relationship? Sally also indicated that she would feel rejected if the counselor did not accept her gift. Would this influence your actions in this case? Sally also indicated a wish to develop a closer relationship with the counselor through giving a gift. How would this influence your decision in this case?

Consider this situation in light of the cultural dimensions. In his article, "Multicultural Perspectives on Multiple Relationships," D. W. Sue (1997) writes: "Additionally, gift giving is a common practice in many Asian communities to show gratitude, respect, and the sealing of a relationship. Such actions are culturally appropriate, yet counselors unfamiliar with such practice may feel that it is inappropriate to accept a gift because it blurs boundaries, changes the relationship, and creates a conflict of interest. They may politely refuse the gift, not realizing the great insult and cultural meaning of their refusal for the giver" (p. 107).

REFERENCES

Herlihy, B., & Corey, G. (1997a). *Boundary issues in counseling: Multiple roles and responsibilities*. Alexandria, VA: American Counseling Association.

In this book, the following sections are of particular relevance to the topic explored in the video:
- Accepting Gifts from Clients (pp. 100–101).
- Sue, D. W. _Multicultural Perspectives on Multiple Relationships (pp. 106–109).

SOME KEY POINTS IN RESOLVING ETHICAL DILEMMAS IN MULTIPLE ROLE SITUATIONS

The main aspect in managing multiple relationships consists of developing safeguards to minimize risks to clients. It is the professional's responsibility to assess for potential negative consequences and to develop measures to reduce (if not eliminate) the potential for harm. These include the following:

- Set healthy boundaries from the outset of a professional relationship.
- To the extent that is possible and appropriate, involve the client in setting the boundaries of the professional relationship.
- Informed consent is essential from the beginning and during the therapeutic relationship.
- If potential dual or multiple relationship problems do occur during the professional relationship, it is essential to assess the risks and benefits associated with the expanding of boundaries.
- Before proceeding with a dual or multiple relationship, it should be clear that there are more benefits than potential risks.
- In order for you to assess the situation, consultation with fellow professionals can be useful in gaining an objective perspective and identifying unanticipated difficulties. Realize that you don't need to make a decision alone.
- Involve the client in an ongoing discussion and in the decision-making process. Document your discussions.
- It is a good idea to give careful thought prior to engaging in a multiple relationship. Don't decide immediately, but let the client know that you want to consult with others and to reflect on the situation. Give careful thought to the potential complications before you get entangled in ethically questionable relationships.
- When dual relationships are potentially problematic, or when the risk for harm is high, it is always wise to work under supervision.
- Again, document in your clinical case notes the nature of this supervision. It is a good idea to keep a record of any actions taken to minimize the risk of harm.
- Throughout the process, self-monitoring is critical. It is good to ask yourself whose needs are being met.

REFERENCES

Albright, D. E., & Hazler, R. J. (1995). A right to die? Ethical dilemmas of euthanasia. *Counseling and Values, 39(3)*, 177–189.

American Association for Marriage and Family Therapy. (1991). *AAMFT code of ethics.* Washington, D.C.: Author.

American Counseling Assocation. (l995). *Code of ethics and standards of practice.* Alexandria, VA: Author.

American Psychological Association. (1995). *Ethical principles of psychologists and code of conduct.* Washington, D.C.: Author.

American Psychological Association. (1993). Guidelines for providers of psychological services to ethnic, linguistic, and culturally diverse populations. *American Psychologist, 48(1),* 45–48.

Anderson, B. S. (1996). *The counselor and the law* (4th ed.). Alexandria, VA: American Counseling Association.

Corey, G. (1996). *Theory and practice of counseling and psychotherapy* (5th ed.). Pacific Grove, CA: Brooks/Cole Publishing.

Corey, G., Corey, C., & Corey, H. (1997). *Living and learning.* Belmont, CA: Wadsworth Publishing Company.

Corey, G., Corey, M., & Callanan, P. (1998) *Issues and ethics in the helping professions* (5th ed.). Pacific Grove, CA: Brooks/Cole Publishing.

Corey, G., & Herlihy, B. (1996a). Client rights and informed consent. In B. Herlihy & G. Corey (Eds.), *ACA ethical standards casebook* (5th ed.) (pp. 181–183). Alexandria, VA: American Counseling Association.

Corey, G., & Herlihy, B. (1996b). Competence. In B. Herlihy & G. Corey (Eds.), *ACA ethical standards casebook* (5th ed.) (pp. 217–220). Alexandria, VA: American Counseling Association.

Corey, G., & Herlihy, B. (1996c). Counselor training and supervision. In B. Herlihy & G. Corey (Eds.), *ACA ethical standards casebook* (5th ed.) (pp. 275–278). Alexandria, VA: American Counseling Association.

Corey, G., & Herlihy, B. (1997). Dual/multiple relationships: Toward a consensus of thinking. In *The Hatherleigh guide to ethics in therapy* (pp. 193–205). New York: Hatherleigh Press.

Corey, M., & Corey, G. (1997). *Groups: Process and practice* (5th ed.). Pacific Grove, CA: Brooks/Cole Publishing.

Corey, M., & Corey, G. (1998) *Becoming a helper* (3rd ed.). Pacific Grove, CA: Brooks/Cole Publishing.

Forester-Miller, H. (1997). Rural communities: Can dual relationships be avoided? In B. Herlihy & G. Corey (1997), *Boundary issues in counseling: Multiple roles and responsibilites* (pp. 99–100). Alexandria, VA: American Counseling Association.

Gill-Wigal, J., & Heaton, J. A. (1996, Summer). Managing sexual attraction in the therapeutic relationship. *Directions in Mental Health Counseling, 6*, 3–14.

Gladding, S.T., Pederson, P., & Stone, D. (1997). Multicultural counseling competencies: A self examination. *ACES Spectrum Newsletter, 58(2)*, 4–5.

Glosoff, H. L. (1997). Multiple relationships in private practice. In B. Herlihy & G. Corey (1997), *Boundary issues in counseling: Multiple roles and responsibilites* (pp. 114–120). Alexandria, VA: American Counseling Association.

Haas, L. J., Malouf, J. L., & Mayerson, N. H. (1986). Ethical dilemmas in psychological practice: Results of a national survey. *Professional Psychology: Research and Practice, 17(4)*, 316–321.

Hatherleigh guide to ethics in therapy. (1997). New York: Hatherleigh Press.

Haynes, R. (1997). Managing multiple relationships in a forensic setting. In B. Herlihy & G. Corey (1997), *Boundary issues in counseling: Multiple roles and responsibilites* (pp. 138–140). Alexandria, VA: American Counseling Association.

Herlihy, B., & Corey, G. (1996a). *ACA ethical standards casebook* (5th ed.). Alexandria, VA: American Counseling Association.

Herlihy, B., & Corey, G. (1996b). Confidentiality. In B. Herlihy & G. Corey (Eds.), *ACA ethical standards casebook* (5th ed.) (pp. 205–209). Alexandria, VA: American Counseling Association.

Herlihy, B., & Corey, G. (1996c). Working with multiple clients. In B. Herlihy & G. Corey (Eds.), *ACA ethical standards casebook* (5th ed.) (pp. 229–233). Alexandria, VA: American Counseling Association.

Herlihy, B., & Corey, G. (1997a). *Boundary issues in counseling: Multiple roles and responsibilities*. Alexandria, VA: American Counseling Association.

Herlihy, B., & Corey, G. (1997b). Codes of ethics as catalysts for improving practice. In *The Hatherleigh guide to ethics in therapy* (pp. 39–59). New York: Hatherleigh Press.

Kitchener, K. S. (1984). Intuition, critical evaluation and ethical principles: The foundation for ethical decisions in counseling psychology. *The Counseling Psychologist, 12(3)*, 43–55.

Kitchener, K.S. (1986). Teaching applied ethics in counselor education: An integration of psychological processes and philosophical analysis. *Journal of Counseling and Development, 64(5)*, 306-310.

Lipsitz, N. E. (1985). *The relationship between ethics training and ethical discrimination ability*. Paper presented at the annual meeting of the American Psychological Association, Los Angeles.

Parham, T. A. (1997). An African-centered view of dual relationships. In B. Herlihy & G. Corey (1997), *Boundary issues in counseling: Multiple roles and responsibilites* (pp. 109–112). Alexandria, VA: American Counseling Association.

Pope, K. S. (1986). New trends in malpractice cases and changes in APA's liability insurance. *Independent Practitioner, 6(4)*, 23–26.

Steinman, S. O., Richardson, N. F., & McEnroe, T. (1998). *The ethical decision-making manual for helping professionals*. Pacific Grove, CA: Brooks/Cole Publishing.

Sue, D.W., Arredondo, P., & McDavis, R.J. (1992). Multicultural counseling competencies and standards: A call to the profession. *Journal of Counseling and Development, 70(4)*, 477–486.

Sue, D. W. (1997). Multicultural perspectives on multiple relationships. In B. Herlihy & G. Corey (1997), *Boundary issues in counseling: Multiple roles and responsibilites* (pp. 106–109). Alexandria, VA: American Counseling Association.

Walden, S. L. (1997). The counselor/client partnership in ethical practice. In B. Herlihy & G. Corey (1997), *Boundary issues in counseling: Multiple roles and responsibilites* (pp. 40–47). Alexandria, VA: American Counseling Association.

Welfel, E. R. (1998). *Ethics in counseling and psychotherapy: Standards, research, and emerging issues.* Pacific Grove, CA: Brooks/Cole Publishing.

Welfel, E. R., & Lipsitz, N. E. (1984). The ethical behavior of professional psychologists: A critical analysis of the research. *The Counseling Psychologist, 12(3),* 31–42.

Wilson, L. S., & Ranft, V. A. (1993). The state of ethical training for counseling psychology doctoral students. *The Counseling Psychologist, 21(3),* 445–456.

OTHER BOOKS BY THE COREYS

The following are other books that the Coreys have authored or co-authored that might be of interest to you. All but *Living and Learning* are published by the Brooks/Cole Publishing Company, Pacific Grove, CA, 93950.

Corey, M. S., & Corey, G. (1998). *Becoming a Helper*, (3rd ed.)

> This book deals with topics of concern to students who are studying in one of the helping professions. Some of the issues explored are examining your motivations and needs, becoming aware of the impact of your values on the counseling process, learning to cope with stress, dealing with burnout, exploring developmental turning points in one's life, and ethical issues.

Corey, G., Corey, M. S., & Callanan, P. (1998). *Issues and Ethics in the Helping Professions*, (5th ed.).

> A combination textbook and student manual that contains self-inventories, open-ended cases and problem situations, exercises, suggested activities, and a variety of ethical, professional, and legal issues facing practitioners.

Corey, G., & Corey, M. S. (1997). *I Never Knew I Had a Choice*, (6th ed.)

> A self-help book for personal growth that deals with topics such as the struggle to achieve autonomy; the roles that work, sex roles, sexuality, love, intimacy, and solitude play in our lives; the meaning of loneliness, death, and loss; and the ways in which we choose values and find meaning in life.

Corey, M. S., & Corey, G. (1997). *Groups: Process and Practice*, (5th ed.)

> Outlines the basic issues and concepts of group process throughout the life history of a group. Applies these basic concepts to groups for children, adolescents, adults, and the elderly.

Corey, G., Corey, C., & Corey, H. (1997). *Living and Learning*. Belmont, CA: Wadsworth.

> Presents learning as a lifelong journey. By encouraging readers to use the world as their classroom and to "learn from living," this book helps readers to get more out of their college experience and the rest of their lives.

Corey, G. (1996). *Theory and Practice of Counseling and Psychotherapy*, (5th ed.)

> Presents an overview of nine contemporary theories of counseling, with an emphasis on the practical applications and the therapeutic process associated

with each orientation. And *Manual for Theory and Practice of Counseling and Psychotherapy*, (5th ed.)

Corey, G. (1996). *Case Approach to Counseling and Psychotherapy*, (4th ed.)

Designed to demonstrate how theory can be applied to specific cases. Outline of theories corresponds to textbook and manual (with the exception of psychodrama). Readers are challenged to apply their knowledge of theories to a variety of cases. Dr. Corey demonstrate his way of working with these cases from each of nine theoretical perspectives and also in an eclectic, integrated fashion. Also, for each of the nine theories there is a central case (Ruth). A proponent of each theory writes about his or her assessment of Ruth and then proceeds to demonstrate his or her particular therapeutic style in counseling Ruth. Dr. Corey follows up by showing how he might intervene with Ruth by staying within the general framework of each of these theories.

Corey, G. (1995). *Theory and Practice of Group Counseling*, (4th ed.)

Presents an overview of ten contemporary theories of counseling applied to group work. And *Manual for Theory and Practice of Group Counseling*, (4th ed.)

Corey, G., Corey, M. S., Callanan, P., & Russell, J. M. (1992). *Group Techniques*, (2nd ed.)

Describes ideas for creating and implementing techniques for use in groups. Gives a rationale for the use of techniques in all the stages in a group's development.

EVALUATION OF *ETHICS IN ACTION: Institutional Version*

We hope you found the video programs useful. We would like to hear from you concerning your evaluation of the value of the programs and your recommendations for us for future video programs that would be useful.

Name _____

Position _____

School _____

Address _____

Phone _____

1. Which videos did you watch?

    ___ Ethics in Action: Institutional Ver.   ___ Ethics in Action: Student Ver.

2. What did you like most about each video?

    Institutional Version _____

    _____

    Student Version _____

    _____

3. What would you have changed about each video?

    Institutional Version _____

    _____

    Student Version _____

    _____

4. Did you use any of the activities or discussion questions from the Facilitator's Resource Manual? Yes ___ No ___

    Were those materials useful? _____

5. What other counseling/therapy video programs would be useful for you to use in the classes you teach? _____

    _____

6. Please add any other comments here. _____

    _____

Thank you for taking time to complete this evaluation. Please return it to Brooks/Cole Publishing Company.

For more information about Brooks/Cole books and videos, please call:

(800) 354-0092

FAX number:
(408) 375-6414

Brooks/Cole Publishing Company
511 Forest Lodge Road
Pacific Grove, CA 93950-9968